WIRED TO LEAD

TO

LEAD

Being the Leader
the Church Didn't Think
You Could Be

SUZANNE NADELL

chalice
PRESS

T0356633

*To young Christian women who are wired to lead
and to the men who are strong enough to support them.
You are not alone.*

Print: 9780827243460

EPUB: 9780827243477

EPDF: 9780827243484

ChalicePress.com

Printed in the United States of America

Contents

Foreword

When I met Suzanne Nadell, I was struck by her sharp mind, witty humor, and depth of conviction. As we worked on her LifePlan©, she shared her story about being a young journalist, driven and eager to make a mark, yet finding herself conflicted in the newsroom because of both her faith and her gender. But Suzanne is a woman who doesn't back down, who uses challenges as fuel to grow, and who finds ways to lead authentically. Like the pages of this book, you'll also learn that much of Suzanne's story is filled with courage and persistence – and a perspective that resonates deeply with female leaders across all walks of life.

In *Wired to Lead*, Suzanne gives voice to so many of us who have wrestled with the complexities of leadership while feeling out of place in the rooms we were born to occupy. From her rural beginnings to winning an Emmy, she shares the hard lessons learned, the challenges faced, and the victories that have shaped her—and through her words, she invites all of us into a transformative conversation about what it truly means to lead as a Christian woman in today's world.

As someone who has spent decades developing female leaders in the church, I understand firsthand how difficult it can be for women to find their place in spaces often marked by invisible barriers. Whether it's the double standards of leadership, the social norms that still favor men, the unconscious biases that shape our opportunities, or the unique practicalities of the journey of womanhood, the road for women is rarely easy. Suzanne bravely tackles these realities with clarity and compassion, while also offering actionable steps for change.

What I appreciate most about Suzanne's leadership—and this book—is her ability to bridge the gap between personal growth and systemic change, and she does it with such passion! She doesn't just point out the problems; she provides solutions rooted in wisdom, faith, and experience. From dismantling biases like Jesus did to paving the way for the next generation of women leaders, Suzanne challenges all of us to rethink our assumptions about leadership, gender, the role of church, and what it means to serve in the Kingdom of God.

One of the most compelling aspects of this book is Suzanne's ability to weave together her professional journey and her spiritual convictions. As someone who has worked in newsrooms and faced the pressures of leadership in a high-stakes environment, Suzanne speaks to the lessons she learned outside the walls of the church—lessons that often stand in stark contrast to the silence or resistance she encountered within them. She calls us, as the church, to be better – not by pointing fingers, but by challenging us to think about what it means for the church to become a place where women are *also* mentored, empowered, and championed to thrive in their God-given callings alongside our brothers.

This book is for every woman who has ever felt sidelined, underestimated, or unqualified simply because of her gender. It is also for every man who has the courage to champion the women in his life and his ministry. It is a call to action for the church to step into its role as a catalyst for justice, equality, and Kingdom-building.

I am honored to be cheering on Suzanne in this work and to recommend this book to you. Whether you are a seasoned leader or just beginning your journey, *Wired to Lead* will challenge and inspire you to step into the fullness of your calling. Let these pages ignite in you the same courage she has developed to lead with faith, wisdom, and love in every room God has called you to lead.

To Suzanne: Thank you for your courage, your voice, and your unwavering commitment to justice and truth. The church—and the world—are better because of leaders like you.

Kadi Cole
Executive Coach, Leadership Consultant &
Author of *Developing Female Leaders*
kadicole.com

Introduction

If we introduced ourselves, you'd quickly learn that I love my job as a journalist and that I'm a Christian. Yes, I'm a Christian and a journalist. And yes, it's possible to be both. Am I a unicorn? No, not really. I've been in the industry since 1995; and while some media sources are agenda-driven, many really are driven by truth.

You might wonder: Is it hard to be a Christian and a journalist? Yes, sometimes it *is* hard. But it's just as hard to be a Christian teacher, nurse, or secretary. Being a *Christian* is what can be hard.

Unfortunately, such introductions often lead us off on political and gender tangents. These often stem from theological leanings that isolate and disqualify people—particularly women—from fulfilling their God-given gifts in a world that needs *all* Christians to stand up for the right things.

Inevitably, such tangents lead to another question: *Why would someone like you go into journalism?* For me, it's all connected to the roles of women in the church.

Let me back up and tell you my story. I'm a "preacher's kid," or PK, from a small town. My dad spent more than forty years in full-time ministry. He was going to be a farmer, but one year into agricultural school he received an anonymous scholarship to a Bible college. My dad loved growing things, but his focus shifted to growing people. Early on, he did some church planting. Later, he led congregations in rural Illinois and Missouri. While I know he aspired to lead bigger churches, he and my mom decided to settle to let their kids grow up in one town. My hometown is Neoga, Illinois. The population is less than two thousand people. I can't speak for what others thought of us, but I never felt like a transplant. It was my home. I had great friends. I love them and their families to this day. In Neoga I will always be referred to as "Suzy Lake" as well as Ron and Donna's daughter and Paul and Sarah's sister.

Neoga is also where I watched my dad lead. My dad doesn't merely *enjoy* growing things (and people): he's really good at it. He's a supporter and a shepherd who knows exactly what to say when people are suffering. He takes pride in researching and writing every sermon he delivers, and he understands "calling on people" (visitation) as fundamental to being a minister. My dad is driven, yet he always feels that there is more he could have done. While I learned and inherited a lot from my mom (a servant's heart, a penchant for gift-giving, and an extremely hard work ethic), I've always been my dad's girl. I look like him; I act like him; and, in his words, I am "wired to lead," just like him.

But as I grew up, it was clear that following in my dad's footsteps was never an option because my church didn't accept having women in leadership. I vividly remember hearing discussions between my dad and people in our congregation focused on whether it was right for women to work part time, let alone lead men in Sunday school. Fortunately, I did see such leadership as I grew up, but in our church women were not deacons or elders and certainly not ministers. I quickly realized my church community believed my only options were to be a preacher's wife or a children's minister. I admit that I resented that and that I spoke (loudly) about not wanting to be a preacher's wife. I didn't want to move around a lot as pastors often do. And I was vocal about not wanting to be a teacher, nurse, or secretary either. In my experience those were the professions of preachers' wives, and since I was not going to be a preacher's wife those were not jobs for me. Though I like kids, it was clear to everyone, including myself, that I should not be a children's minister.

This led me to obsess over one driving question: *What should I be?* In junior high school, I declared I would be an attorney. Then, during my freshman year, a new passion began developing in my heart. I started watching *20/20* with my dad on Friday nights—the old Hugh Downs and Barbara Walters version of *20/20*. I loved Hugh and Barbara, the stories they told, and that they uncovered who was behind bad things.

I decided I was going into TV news, and I made sure everyone knew it.

That summer I attended a Christ in Youth conference with my youth group at Milligan College in Johnson City, Tennessee. Milligan is a Christian liberal arts college affiliated with the movement in which I grew up. One of its early leaders is quoted as describing Christian education as the "hope of the world"—meaning that you need Christians of *all* professions to make an impact. This includes *all* media outlets, not just the Christian ones. The college's communications program had a broadcasting and journalism concentration. It made an impression on me, and I knew I had found my place. I remember announcing to my youth group friends and leaders that had I decided I was going to attend Milligan and major in communications. And that's exactly what I did.

It was 1995 when I first set foot in a TV newsroom. While a sophomore at Milligan, one of its alumni gave me my first job as a production assistant. I subsequently became a producer and reporter, all before graduating from college. After graduation I went the producing route, moving across the country and into management. Today I am the news director of the top local station in the country. I've seen ratings success and built newsrooms; and my office is filled with Edward R. Murrow, Emmy, and Associated Press awards. Television news embraced me, and I excelled.

As I developed as an industry leader, however, my soul became increasingly unsettled. At one point, resentment set in. Though I am wired to lead, though I knew I had something to offer and I wanted to give my all, my all wasn't accepted in the church—simply because I am a woman. That was the heart of my struggle. I subconsciously determined that if the church wasn't going to accept all of me, it wasn't going to get all of me.

While I did stay connected and continued to grow in faith, my focus became my career. During that time some ill-informed Christians wondered aloud how I could be a Christian *and* be part of the media. But I learned valuable kingdom lessons in newsrooms. Some of those lessons came from fellow Christians there. Other lessons came from people who may not consider themselves to be Christians but believe wholeheartedly in justice, service, and love. Other lessons came simply by getting out of my comfy bubble of people who think exactly like I do and becoming the hands and feet of Jesus. A great many lessons I learned by messing up and from amazing leaders who understood good principles of leading and who spoke candidly to me in love. They were my advocates. They taught me to do the right thing always. They taught me how to respect others and stay out of compromising situations. And yes, they taught me how to navigate the "boys' club" of upper management.

Some people might say my life has worked out the way God planned, regardless of those who discouraged me or tried to hold me back. And perhaps it has. Others have told me I have reached more people by leading a newsroom than I would have reached from a pulpit. Perhaps they're right. But imagine how much the world would change if we empowered our young female leaders in the church as much as we do our boys. Imagine how strong we could be by doubling our people investment. If we championed our girls, that's what we would be doing.

Sadly, the church was not always there to mentor me in ways in which those outside the church were. And I am not alone. Have you experienced loneliness, confusion, or even abandonment in your church because you are female or because your career path didn't fit people's expectations? This isn't right, and I believe it is high time for the church to be there for you. I believe God has called you to be more than a wife. Women who are born and wired to lead should be able to lead, and they should not have to go outside the church to do so. If God calls you outside the church, great. But perhaps God is calling you to lead *in* the church, just like your fathers, brothers, and male friends.

Dear church, it is time to step up! In newsrooms we are held to a high fact-checking standard. It's time to fact-check our thoughts, approaches, and even agendas as believers in Jesus Christ and as his ambassadors to the world. It's time we are there to support and teach young women the lessons I had to learn outside the church's walls. Let's enter into a discussion about the lessons I should have learned from the church. And let's get it right for the girls and women coming after me.

Together, We Can Make a Change

Throughout this book I share examples and stories of the lessons I learned in the marketplace. I then share action items for you to set these lessons in motion in your personal life or in the ministry to young women in your church.

What I say might prompt you to question your opinion or theology about the biblical role of women in the church. It's okay if you don't agree with me. But I do want to make you think.

This book is primarily for women wired to lead who want to know how they can use their gifts for the glory of God, no matter where their church stands on the issue.

It is written for those who believe there are opportunities for women in the church and in the marketplace and who want to make sure our girls and young women are equipped to embrace them.

In addition to the reflection questions, you'll see the book is broken into four sections. We're going to explore everything from justice and ethics, bridging the gender divide, taking care of yourself, and how you can help be the solution. These are areas in which newsrooms taught me valuable life lessons—lessons I wish I had learned in church. My hope is this book will prompt thought and discussion in small reflection groups and book clubs and among church leaders.

I don't believe it's a coincidence that the "#MeToo" movement along with increased attention to racial injustice are happening within years of each other. It's time for the church to stop being silent about these matters. It is time for the church to hear all the voices in the room. We in the church are alienating our children by limiting what we allow them to do. And when we do so, they will go somewhere else for acceptance. Let's be there for them. Let's hear them. And let's get out of our comfy bubble and make some real change in this world.

I am cheering you on.

— *Suzanne*

SECTION 1

Justice and Ethics
According to Jesus

Dismantle Unconscious Biases Like Jesus Did

I was working in an Atlanta newsroom during the fallout of the murder of George Floyd. A peaceful protest in our city led to a violent night of looting and vandalism, which led to a week of nightly protests. The governor called in the National Guard and police to maintain order. Just as that ended, an unarmed man named Rayshard Brooks died when police shot him as he ran away. The city erupted. The restaurant where the shooting happened was torched.

I have been in other newsrooms when black men were shot and killed by police. I also worked the night eight people died in two cities in metro Atlanta because a man who claimed to be a Christian said he was trying to eliminate sexual temptation by gunning down Asian women.

I have been part of passionate exchanges in newsrooms—exchanges about what information is relevant to a story; what is enough source information to report; what details are not necessary to convey the story adequately; what thoughts, statements, or perspectives only feed a narrative that we already know isn't true.

Then there are the opinions that surface about the particulars. Do past drug charges have anything to do with a man being shot in the back by a police officer? Or do those past drug charges explain why he ran? Does voicing such information plant a narrative seed in the community: "See, he's a bad guy"? Is bringing up a decade-old prostitution charge involving a woman who was gunned down at a spa relevant to the story? Or does that feed a narrative created by a system that sexualizes Asian women only to victimize them again, even in their death?

Anyone who thinks such discussions and the decisions on what to report are taken lightly hasn't been in any newsroom of which I've been a part. It's in covering such stories that I've learned about the power of unconscious bias and the devastating role it plays in discriminating against others, usually because of that person's race or gender.

Lessons Learned about Becoming Aware of Our Biases

It pains me that I did not learn about unconscious biases in the church. I cannot remember a single occasion on which a preacher addressed bias and equality from the pulpit or a Sunday school teacher taught about it in one of my childhood classes. However, I applaud my parents for addressing racial prejudice in our house. My dad, who went to Bible college in a diverse city in the 1960s, had a roommate named Robby, a Black man from Barbados. He and his family were always part of our lives. My dad told stories of situations in which Robby had been discriminated against and how even people my dad loved had reacted poorly when he brought his roommate home to visit. It still grieved him years later, and he made sure we kids knew discrimination is wrong.

My dad had no tolerance for people using certain words around us to describe people of color. I vividly remember him shutting down a family member for using the N-word. My dad was well-versed in the civil rights movement, and when anyone brought someone diverse to our town or church, he made them feel welcome. After those visits, he explained to us the difficulties such folks often face in small, homogenous towns like ours and how he felt for them.

The subject that didn't come up in these conversations was the inequality some people face due to discrimination. The "why" behind people's actions he never discussed, with the exception of explaining why some people described some people of color as "good ones," a description I never heard others use of white people. This created a narrative in my mind that I did not even realize existed until I was in my forties. Because my parents were very loving, accepting, and understanding compared to many people I knew, I thought I understood how to make a difference and combat racial injustice. Because people in my church opened their arms to Robby and his son when they visited from Barbados, I thought I was surrounded by nice people. I remained oblivious to the discrimination many people of color face every day—even from these otherwise kind, well-intentioned people.

It wasn't until after the 2017 Charlottesville, Virginia, "Unite the Right rally" of white supremacist organizations that I heard a pastor of a church I attended say: "This is wrong." Toney stood on stage that Sunday, after all of America had watched scenes of Nazi flags flying and KKK members marching, and boldly said that as Christians we cannot be silent about this atrocity toward God's children. He was right. Nothing about that rally represented what Jesus taught us to do when he commanded us to love each other as he first loved us. Furthermore, sitting and watching it while claiming that some of the people in the crowds that day were "good people," and that the media members sensationalized the messages of hate, was just as wrong as actively participating in the march itself.

Toney's proclamation of truth sat deeply in my soul. It still does. Yet I was sad I had never heard that message at church camps, conferences, Sunday school, and sermons in the previous four decades of my life. I could attempt to justify my ignorance or lack of backbone by saying I'd grown up in a different time and that back then we honestly did think we were "good people." I could try to justify my inaction by reminding myself that no amount of sadness, remorse, or non-active engagement in hateful or sinful behavior toward others changes what took place in the past. That's the argument to which many well-intentioned, "good" Christians resort when they don't want to consider the truth in the criticism. But moving forward we can—and should—take more responsibility. Let's change what we tell our children in the church today. In fact, let's lead the way in these conversations. Galatians 3:26–28 should be a passage we talk about with our children so they understand the equality and unity God designed for *all* of humankind. Let's not gloss over it as if it were less important than other aspects of our biblical worldview. Let's really talk about it and help our children (and fellow adults) understand how valuable *everyone* is to God.

> So in Christ Jesus you are all children of God through faith, for all of you who were baptized into Christ have clothed yourselves with Christ. There is neither Jew nor Gentile, neither slave nor free, nor is there male and female, for you are all one in Christ Jesus (NIV).

I learned the truth of this verse from reporting some difficult news stories, from mistakes I and others have made, and from some people who were brave enough not only to call me out for my unconscious biases but also to help me become better.

While I was leading a newsroom in Pittsburgh, I learned one of my hardest and most valuable lessons about unconscious bias. A very reputable source and numerous confirmations brought to light information in a story involving a young man whom a police officer had shot fatally in the back. The story was already drawing national attention because the teen was running away when the cop took aim. I was returning from vacation at the time, and when I got off the plane a newsroom leader called to tell me they had information that implied the teen had fired a gun at the officer. Journalistically, our team had followed all the steps. We had an appropriate number of sources corroborating our story who were well-connected to the information shared, and we involved multiple managers in reviewing all the information and making the decision to move forward with reporting the story. We had ample information confirming our reporting. Other sources said our information was wrong. But our sources maintained that what they had told was true, and they said those conflicting sources were just caught up in semantics and we had nothing to worry about.

However, some of the information we presented did end up being incorrect. There was no video of the teen firing a gun. I remember feeling sick to my stomach when this became clear. I remember wondering whether some people could be so dead set on supporting their agenda that they would lie to the media, burning relationships by changing the plot of a story.

That weekend I pulled aside a church elder who is black. I told him what had unfolded. He replied: "I don't think they intentionally lied to you. People see what they want to see."

I have kept that powerful statement with me: "People see what they want to see." It is the perfect definition of unconscious bias.

On the website *Simply Psychology*, writer Charlotte Ruhl explains that the term "implicit bias," or unconscious bias, was first coined in 1995 by psychologists Mahzarin Banaji and Anthony Greenwald, who argued that social behavior is largely influenced by unconscious associations and judgments.

Ruhl breaks down this concept into simple explanations she calls "Take Home Messages" for us to understand and manage biases. Implicit biases are unconscious attitudes and stereotypes that can manifest anywhere, but perhaps most harmfully in the criminal justice system, workplace, school setting, and the health care system.

1. Implicit bias is also known as unconscious bias or implicit social cognition.
2. There are many different examples of implicit biases, ranging from categories of race, gender, and sexuality.
3. These biases often arise as a result of trying to find patterns and navigate the overwhelming stimuli in this very complicated world. Culture, media, and upbringing can also contribute to the development of such biases.
4. Removing these biases is a challenge, especially because we often don't even know they exist, but research suggests hope that levels of implicit biases in the United States are decreasing.[1]

---

[1] Charlotte Ruhl, "Implicit Unconscious Bias," *Simply Psychology*, July 1, 2020, https://www.simplypsychology.org/implicit-bias.html.

I appreciate Ruhl's last takeaway. She uses the word "intervention" to describe what might be leading to decreasing levels of biases. Thanks to her, I now understand past conversations with church leaders, coworkers, and friends as interventions in my life. Each of these people was brave enough to call out my actions and demand that I reflect on why I did what I did or believed what I believed.

Recognizing my unconscious biases only happened when I was able to examine my thoughts and actions candidly by opening myself to conversations with people who pushed me to understand how my thoughts—conscious and unconscious—affect my words, decisions, and actions. And now that I *know* better, it's up to me to *do* better.

One area in which I fed a bias in my workplace was my dealings with women's hair. In many newsrooms across the country, natural hair, especially for women of color, is considered unprofessional and even distracting to viewers. I was more lenient than many newsroom leaders in asking that each person be consistent in how they styled their hair. But I hadn't taken the time to understand the emotional and physical toll that took on some women who felt pressure to straighten their hair. I now know that, over time, scores of female journalists, including some who worked for me, endured their hair falling out as a result of such treatments and styling. Many white people don't understand that "twists" or "braids" are not solely a fashion statement; they are also "protective styles" created to prevent damage from weather and harsh "beauty" treatments.

I have very thick curly, coarse hair, and peers have advised me to keep it straight to boost my "executive presence." While doing so is difficult and costly, I can fairly easily get a blowout. Such straightening is nothing like the chemicals and heat needed to straighten Black hair. And while I applaud Black women for encouraging women to embrace their natural beauty and accept themselves, white women like me should not put their hair struggles in the same category. Our societal pressures do not come close to meeting a Black woman's pressure to meet Eurocentric beauty standards. Racial injustice and unconscious bias have permeated all levels of society—even our hair. Women are constantly being told they must look a certain way to meet basic (white) standards of beauty.

What has made all these matters worse is that we rarely listen to other viewpoints. We don't stop to listen to our conscience telling us that such a rule about hair is unfair, nor do we listen to our colleague's complaints or concerns. We rarely listen to people, let alone try to understand those who have struggles or perceptions that differ from ours. We let our unconscious biases get in the way. We convince ourselves that because we are required to look a certain way, others should be required to play by the same rules. We convince ourselves that some victims of violence, including violence involving police officers, must be bad people. We convince ourselves that it is only through our own hard work and because we deserve it that we've reached our professional goals. We don't listen to those who are "not like us." We don't listen to others' experiences. This failure to listen and these convictions and choices fuel unconscious biases.

Lessons Learned about Acting on Your Knowledge

I am forever grateful to my colleagues of color who called me out, who said, "Suzanne, now that you know X, what are you going to do about it?"

Dear church, once you know the truth about your biases, what are you going to do about it? Jesus spent his time on earth with people in the margins establishing justice and helping the oppressed. That is what being a Christian is about. Sadly, I have felt called to that mission in a newsroom more than I have inside the walls of a church because many churches are uncomfortable with the idea of getting uncomfortable. We Christians don't want to challenge our thinking or admit we might be part of the problem. Frankly, we're self-righteous. And while there are probably some people in every congregation who are willing to take the uncomfortable steps required to change, there are just as many who are afraid someone will get offended and leave if the church takes a stand for justice and changes the way things "have always been." It's easier to keep doing things the way we always have. But Jesus and Paul call us to be bridges to reconciliation. In 2 Corinthians 5:14-21 Paul talks about this ministry of reconciliation:

For Christ's love compels us, because we are convinced that one died for all, and therefore all died. And he died for all, that those who live should no longer live for themselves but for him who died for them and was raised again. So from now on we regard no one from a worldly point of view. Though we once regarded Christ in this way, we do so no longer. Therefore, if anyone is in Christ, the new creation has come: The old has gone, the new is here! All this is from God, who reconciled us to himself through Christ and gave us the ministry of reconciliation: that God was reconciling the world to himself in Christ, not counting people's sins against them. And he has committed to us the message of reconciliation. We are therefore Christ's ambassadors, as though God were making his appeal through us. We implore you on Christ's behalf: Be reconciled to God. God made him who had no sin to be sin for us, so that in him we might become the righteousness of God (NIV).

A key verse in this passage is verse 14: "Christ's love compels us because we are convinced that one died for all, and therefore all died." As Christians, we should be compelled *by Christ's love of us* to love and share the good news with *everyone*. Our drive shouldn't be based on protecting people who are just like us. God didn't count anyone's sins against them. No one is less worthy of his grace than another. Instead, he came with a message of reconciliation for all. Imagine the good we, the church, could do if we focused on being ambassadors of Christ's message. Imagine what would happen if we took the time to see with our hearts.

If you feel as if you are on the fringes, or if you are frightened by the idea of opening up opportunities to everyone, maybe you are too far from the margins. Maybe you are living inside your comfy bubble of people who look like you, think like you, and don't challenge your line of thinking. Christ calls us to live out *all* that he told us to do. Christ charged us to be ambassadors of the message that in Christ we are *all* one. We are *all* sinners. And Christ calls us *all* to the ministry of reconciliation.

I felt that call to the ministry of reconciliation through people I met at work, not church. It is through those relationships that I have learned of my role in preserving and strengthening these unconscious biases and of the privilege I had previously never consciously realized I had.

Lessons Learned about My Privilege

Some of you may be questioning why you are even reading this book. You may be thinking, "Suzanne is a liberal journalist disguised as a Christian who tricked me into reading a book that discusses white privilege." You may even be one of the many people who believe the term "white privilege" is racist. It's not. When you really understand it, you realize it doesn't mean "anti-white people." It's a term that describes a reality of our society. If you are white, you have experienced privilege. Even if life has been hard for you and even if you don't know it, you have had some—and probably many—privileges that black people are not afforded. Think about your education, your access to fresh and healthy food and to good and affordable health care. Think about the times you have been stopped by police. Did you fear for your life? Do you fear for your son's life every time he leaves the house? Think about the books you read in school, perhaps long ago. Did you study any non-white artists, philosophers, novelists, scientists, musicians? What unconscious norms were you taught? Was it challenging to get your first bank account, loan, or mortgage? Did the tone of real estate agents change when they saw the color of your skin? Has anyone ever rushed to lock their car door or cross the street because they saw you walking in their direction? I encourage you to study the topic objectively. Engage in constructive conversations with others who have opinions and information about privilege—or lack of it. Partner with someone who wants to use knowledge and conversation, and help each other grow. It helped me, and it may help you.

Understanding what white privilege is and identifying your own privilege is hard and often painful work. It means taking an honest look at yourself and your past to admit the advantages you experience. And it means doing something to shift the imbalances of power and privilege in society—in your family, neighborhood, state, church, school, country.

According to 2019 U.S. Census data, the average per capita income in my hometown was less than $25,000 a year.[2] Yet even though I did not come from money, I was privileged—had advantages—simply because I am white. I worked as a teen, and I worked full time through college. I bought my first car through a loan. I did not pay off my college loans until I was forty-one. And I really believed that because I had made it, anyone could. I denied having white privilege, was even unconscious of it. Yes, I worked. Pat me on the back! But the difference lies in the fact that my work was at my own will and determination. I didn't have to work too hard to get what I wanted. And every opportunity I chased was mine to grasp.

I was offered a job at Wendy's "on the spot" when I was sixteen, with no experience. I got a loan for a car at my small town's bank when I was sixteen thanks to my parents' good credit and them cosigning for the loan. I had access to the loans needed to go to the school of my choice, and I got any part-time or full-time job to which I applied to pay my way through. My professors at my Christian liberal arts college were able to pick up the phone to the general manager and news director of the TV station in town and tell them they would not regret hiring me. Because of those connections, I was able to graduate from college with a poor GPA because I had worked so much but with more than two years' full-time TV experience, some even on camera, which enabled me to land a great job right out of college. When I was financially irresponsible in my young adult years, there were people to bail me out. A car dealer even went out of his way to help me get a car loan when my credit was in the toilet.

Did I work hard? Yes. Did I have some natural talent and skills? Yes. Did I deserve a second chance when I was so exhausted from working multiple jobs and my self-esteem was so depleted that I thought material things would make me happy and I put myself in

---

[2] "Neoga, Illinois Income Map, Earnings Map, and Wages Data," *City-Data*, accessed January 31, 2022, https://www.city-data.com/income/income-Neoga-Illinois.html.

debt even though I could not pay my bills? Yes, I thought I did. And I got more than one second chance. Did anyone ever regret hiring me or giving me a reference? Nope.

Those things are all true. Yet I have learned that many equally talented people of color would not have had all those chances. I can pat myself on the back for everything I have done that has led to my success—and it is a lot—but I cannot deny that I have had opportunities unavailable to most people of color.

The saddest part of this is that I learned this lesson in the marketplace, not in church. Indeed, many Christians have fed unconscious biases by assuming we understand the plight of others and by not encouraging diversity in our congregations and social circles. Shame on us! It is time for the church to take ownership in this area and lead the ministry of reconciliation.

I am far from perfect in this area, but I am learning thanks to some amazing women who have helped me understand the hurtful inequity in our society. I now know that I will *never* have to take my son to introduce him to our new neighbors when moving into a neighborhood so they know he lives there and is not there to cause trouble. I work with women who live a life where that is what they must do. And sadly, they also have to tell their kids not to wear hoodies or how to act when being pulled over. I will *never* have to do that either. While acknowledging this to a coworker, she said: "This is great. It's going to take white awakened women to awaken other white women." Yes, it will. So, dear church, what are we going to do about it?

Lessons Learned about Uncomfortable Conversations

What can the church do? Well, I believe we must start by talking about this. Nothing will happen without taking that first step. Honest conversations will be uncomfortable, and that's okay because discomfort leads to vulnerability and transformation. You've probably heard the saying "nothing grows in a comfort zone." I believe that to be particularly true when it comes to reconciliation. Create opportunities for dialogue. Then, when you invite someone who doesn't look like you to open up, try listening more than speaking.

We also have to invite people who are not like us inside our social circles, churches, and communities. Dr. Martin Luther King Jr. said the most segregated hour in the week is 11 o'clock on Sundays.[3] We can save for another day the debate on why that is because you and I both know that's a whole different book on a topic that deserves a lot more attention than I could possibly give it here. Suffice it to say that you might have to make a deliberate effort to surround yourself and your children with people who are unlike you—and that is necessary if you really want to understand and love your neighbors.

Christians have become masters at creating their own comfy circles. Jesus challenged the thinking of everyone around him—from his interactions with the woman at the well to the story of the good Samaritan. He even dragged the disciples along with him to sit at the table with a tax collector to show us we are all sons and daughters of the King. Who have you let inside your circles to challenge your thinking? Whom do you unconsciously not consider an equal son or daughter of the King?

I vividly remember my youth group going to a predominantly black church to sing. That congregation was so welcoming. It was a great experience. My youth group leaders were on the right track. They showed us there are people who don't look like us and churches that don't worship like us but love God as much as we do. They also showed us that at the end of the day we all have the same goals to love God and love people. The problem was that the conversations centered around stereotypes based on traditions, attire for church, or styles of worship took place before and after our visit because of a lack of exposure to diversity. And since we weren't surrounded by people of diversity, nobody was around to explain why those traditions existed or how they were to be celebrated, no matter how different they were from our own.

The marketplace has done a great job at making diversity and inclusion a priority. Businesses partner with organizations, pursue

---

[3] *Meet the Press,* "Martin Luther King Jr. The Most Segregated Hour in America," *Meet the Press,* April 17, 1960, posted April 29, 2014, YouTube video, https://www.youtube.com/watch?v=1q881g1L_d8.

create initiatives, and bring in experts to help make it happen. Maybe the church can take a page out of that playbook. Partner with another church from another part of town. Bring in a facilitator for honest and open conversations with church leaders and groups. Be prepared to be uncomfortable. Have uncomfortable conversations. Maybe then we can grow to be the ambassadors in the ministry of reconciliation.

I like to imagine what "on earth as it is in heaven" would look like. In heaven we have no fear. We are all God's children. I think we should return to looking at things as children do. They don't possess any unconscious biases; they just see people as people. Wouldn't it be awesome if it were that way with adults? Wouldn't it be awesome if the church led the way instead of making earth different than heaven?

ACTION ITEMS

1. Look into organizations like Be the Bridge. which states its belief that complete racial unity and justice cannot happen apart from the reconciling work of Jesus Christ on the cross and the power of the Holy Spirit to move individuals to make peace with God and all humankind.[4] They train people to be "bridge builders." Organizations like this one are dedicated to helping the church "be the bridge" in racial inequality.

2. Ask yourself when the last time was that you made a diversified hire or went out of your way to add diversity to your leadership team. The marketplace has led in this, but the church has a long way to go. When looking to add diversity on your team, it's important that you realize some diverse candidates might not have had previous opportunities, so they might not seem as qualified. Give people a chance, and fully support them once they are in the door. We all need diversity in the room to bridge this gap.

---

[4] "About Be the Bridge," *Be the Bridge*, accessed January 29, 2022, https://bethebridge.com/about/.

3. Find a cultural/diversity partner. After the murder of George Floyd, I realized some of my unconscious biases. I was talking this out with a diverse leader at my TV station, and out of nowhere she said, "I'll be your cultural/diversity partner." She and another diverse coworker, who unofficially became a partner of mine, became my safe spaces. I needed people who were diverse with whom I could speak openly without feeling judged. I also needed to be called out in love. If you don't have diversity in your church to facilitate this, work with another organization or another church. And if you are a leader, start with yourself.

4. Read as much as you can on the matter. The first assignments made by my cultural/diversity partner were reading assignments—lots of books and eventually some documentaries. Reading can illuminate inadequacy and probably make you feel uncomfortable. Be okay with being uncomfortable and realizing you have messed up. Then take what you've learned and help others be better.

Self-Reflection Questions for Church Leaders

1. How have you discussed unconscious biases in your church?

2. How have unconscious biases stopped you from being the hands and feet of Jesus?

3. Are there any instances in which your leadership team has "seen what they wanted to see"?

4. How have you facilitated conversations about privilege and the impact it may have had on your church's decisions?

5. Do you create "safe spaces" for uncomfortable conversations?

Self-Reflection Questions for Female Leaders

1. Have you thought about your unconscious biases?

2. Who in your inner circle can call you out on your unconscious biases?

3. When have you "seen what you wanted to see," and what did it cost you or others?

4. What would make you more comfortable having uncomfortable conversations so you can grow?

5. How has privilege helped you in ways you might not have realized previously?

Love *All* Your Neighbors

"Love your neighbor as yourself." —*Mark 12:31 (NIV)*

If you do a quick Google search for Bible verses about loving your neighbor, you'll find dozens. In the verse above from the Gospel of Mark, Jesus refers to loving your neighbor as yourself as the second greatest commandment. Our love for one another is tantamount to the outward expression of our love for God—our first responsibility. Of course, we encounter these truths as we study God's Word and attend church services. We now also encounter them on social media and on cute T-shirts with adorable hearts and Jesus' words in beautiful fonts. Unfortunately, those same social media feeds bring us memes and quotations that express contentious or even unloving sentiments toward others. And our conversations can go the same way—one minute sharing hope and inspiration, the next spewing hatred and prejudice. We constantly send mixed messages if we aren't careful to tame our tongues and keep love at the forefront of our encounters with others.

I think we intend to love others. No one actually tries *not* to love their neighbor, right? But isn't genuinely loving your neighbor difficult? It's easy to say we love our neighbor by signing up for a meal train when they are sick or by going to a homeless shelter once in a while and serving a meal. But after we make our delivery or put in our hour of service, we get to return to our cozy home, physically distancing ourselves by miles—and possibly even mentally distancing ourselves—from the hardship of those we served. We "checked off a box" by doing our good deed. We call this "loving our neighbor"— and it is. But does it express the depth of what Jesus desired when he highlighted how significant a task loving others really is? Are we truly bearing others' burdens and reaping the fruit of all God wants to cultivate in our souls when we check off caring tasks so easily?

Along the same lines, it's easy to love those who agree with us. But what about that neighbor who puts up signs in support of a political candidate with whom we disagree? And what about loving the neighbor who lets their dog do its business in your yard? Such neighbors can be hard to love. Just look at apps people use to share neighborhood news. Though mine has some good examples of people loving their neighbors, the majority of the feed is filled with people openly complaining about their neighbors.

And my question was just about whether you find it difficult to love your neighbors in adverse situations! I didn't even ask how difficult it is for you to love them as *yourself*—which is what Jesus commanded us to do. So be honest: Do you really love that neighbor with the annoying political sign or the one whose dog just went in your yard yet again as much as you love yourself? And do you really love the unhoused person who you see daily standing at the intersection as much as you love yourself?

Perhaps we need to start by identifying whether we even consider that person our "neighbor." Let's begin by asking ourselves the question the Samaritans asked Jesus: "Who is my neighbor?" Through the story of the good Samaritan, Jesus made it clear that the neighbor was "the one showed [the needy man] mercy" (Luke 10:37 NIV).

Sit with Jesus' response for a bit. Jesus didn't say it was the one who lived in his neighborhood. Or the one who went to his church. Or the one who looked like him or believed the way he did. The neighbor is the one who took the time to help someone he didn't know, the one who took the time to help someone despite the likelihood he wouldn't get anything in return, not even a "thank you." Caring for someone in need without any expectation of reciprocity: that's being a neighbor.

Lessons Learned about Serving My Neighbors

While the church in which I grew up provided some opportunities to serve stranded motorists whose cars had broken down on the highways passing through our small town, or to buy Christmas presents for kids who otherwise wouldn't get them, it wasn't until I was employed in the media that I actually started to love my neighbor in the way Jesus expects of us. But most of the efforts in which I have been involved were not connected to my church but to the TV stations at which I worked. Why? Newsrooms are full of people from different backgrounds, neighborhoods, and beliefs, people involved in organizations and processes that can respond quickly to need. These people hear about the needs of people in our entire viewing area, not just in our own neighborhoods. Accordingly, local broadcast stations often lead community relief efforts. I can tell you from personal experience that those efforts aren't just marketing ploys. The Federal Communications Commission license is what allows your local television station to use the free airwaves. In order to maintain that license, stations must document how they serve the community in everything from providing news coverage to sharing life-saving information and engaging in community efforts.

I know many people in local news who have servants' hearts. They work holidays and long hours and risk their lives to cover storms, protests, and violence; and they do it all for a lot less pay than you might think. They do it because they truly love their neighbors. They want to inform, prepare, and warn their neighbors about what's happening in their community and where they can receive help. They do it because they can't imagine not using their gifts of communication and leadership to love their neighbors.

Media members' desire to love their neighbors is something "news kids" understand, too. That's what I affectionately call children of newsroom employees. Their lives are strange ones. Their parents work crazy hours, and they are exposed to behind-the-scenes parts of TV that—while fascinating to adults looking in from the outside—are ordinary for news kids. It's their life.

I'll never forget having to rush to work for tornado coverage in Oklahoma. Our son, Price, was about five years old. He already knew the drill of what to do when there was a tornado warning. It was Oklahoma, after all. But I gave him a hug and, as I headed out the door, I reminded him that he and Daddy knew what to do to stay safe while I helped make sure other moms and little boys stayed safe, too.

Today Price will tell you his mom's job is important; she informs the public. He also will tell you that his mom and many of the people with whom she works do it because they have servants' hearts and that they rush every day to serve people they will never meet because that's what real love does.

Not only do we media people rush to love our neighbors, but newsroom employees do so under a lot of pressure. Most of us are adrenaline junkies. We rarely know for sure what our day will bring, and it typically changes several times a day. But we can handle it. We're people who can work together for good.

I have seen people of faith lead station initiatives that have big impact among neighbors. One such initiative is Convoy of Care, an effort organized by a nonprofit that focuses on helping people in urgent times of need. An Atlanta investigative reporter worked with the nonprofit Caring for Others by connecting them with law enforcement connections he had made during his three decades of investigative coverage. He also used his influence to connect them with a group of truckers.

I've seen Convoy of Care spring into action in a matter of hours after a tornado ripped through a local community and when a hurricane led to a need for clean drinking water in Texas and Haiti. Organizations like Caring for Others are the church without walls moving in the world. You don't always see this depth of care or sense of efficiency within the four walls of the church. Fortunately, organizations like Convoy of Care see a need through reports like ours on TV, and people with servants' hearts rally people together who can pool their resources in mass response to help show mercy to their neighbors. Then a convoy of trucks takes donated supplies to those in need, all in the name of love.

Now, this is where a newsroom has an advantage. Every day we see the impact of devastation and need. We cannot escape it. It is our job to report on it, so it is top of mind. The challenge for us as churches is to get out of our "bubbles" of people who are just like us to see the needs around us and spring into action quickly.

This is where I believe the church can lean on marketplace leaders in their congregations. Marketplace leaders, whether from newsrooms, businesses, or large organizations, are trained to spot big community needs, be visible, organize, and make initiatives happen. How awesome it would be if we churches could be just as visible helping in times of need!

Outsiders misunderstand both newsrooms and churches. Many unchurched people think churches are filled with people who either really don't care or who are out for fame or money. Such unchurched people may have had a bad experience or have never been exposed to a group of Jesus-loving people. This is just like many believers who, because they don't know anyone who works in a newsroom, believe newsrooms are full of people who are opportunistic and agenda-driven for certain political parties. What if the church could learn from the swift and loving response of marketplace businesses, like newsrooms, and be seen as the first responders in times of need? Talk about being the hands and feet of Jesus *and* having influence on the perspectives of unbelievers toward the church! Naturally, as the church, we have only so much influence over unbelievers through our example. The real opportunity is engagement in layers and layers of needs throughout our communities.

For example, take virtual learning during the COVID-19 pandemic.

The exhaustion was real. For me, the first two months I felt as if I was live-producing hurricane coverage from 7:00 a.m. until 7:00 p.m. every day. But you know how I got perspective? An eye-opening call from a superintendent of one of the largest school districts in metro Atlanta. While I and everyone I knew were exhausted, our problems were nothing compared to the challenges the school system was enduring. Many children were starving because they were no longer getting school lunches (sometimes their only meal of the day), as they were unable to pick them up at the designated hand-out times. The number of children who had no access to Internet in our "nner-cities and in rural America was much larger than many people wanted to admit. The superintendent told me of children walking to a neighborhood fast food restaurant to access internet and how this could put their lives in danger because of the violence that can surround them. These children were also often being robbed of their only moment of the day to be truly seen, taught, and inspired by an adult.

The Bellwether Education Partners conducted a study about this very matter. They estimated that between March and October 2020 one to three million children in the U.S. had not attended school. The most at risk were:

1. Students in foster care

2. Students experiencing homelessness

3. English learners

4. Students with disabilities (ages 6–21)

5. Students eligible for the Migrant Education Program[5]

This is not merely an urban issue. The pandemic exposed the disparities in rural America on everything from access to medical care to the lack of internet access for our children. Just a year before the pandemic, a Pew Research study revealed that 63 percent of people in rural America had no broadband at home.[6]

The superintendent on the phone with me that day wasn't disputing the need for virtual remote learning: she was simply trying her best to inform and mobilize people to serve those families in need. Looking back on that situation, I think what a remarkable teachable moment the church missed out on: our children didn't get to see

---

[5] Emily A. Vogels, "Some Digital Divides Persist Between Rural, Urban and Suburban America," *Pew Research Center,* August 19, 2021, https://www. pewresearch.org/fact-tank/2021/08/19/some-digital-divides-persist-between-rural-urban-and-suburban-america/.

[6] Vogels, "Some Digital Divides Persist."

the church come together to prioritize the care of these families in a significant way. I admit that, until I spoke with the superintendent as part of my employment duties, it hadn't crossed my mind that there might be many families who didn't read or speak English well enough to understand the notice we parents received to pick up laptops from school for our children. I can only imagine how much those children missed out on because they couldn't show up for Zoom lessons, while my child was readily and easily engaged.

It takes love to wonder how others with fewer resources and opportunities are affected by these same circumstances. It takes love to seek out the leaders, influencers, and organizations who serve those demographics to see what the real needs are and how we can help. We might not all be able to get appointments with school superintendents and homeless agencies. But what if our church leaders did? What love it would show if we, the church, learned of this need from the superintendents in our communities and stepped out of our comfort zones to check in on one other family who might not have received or been able to understand the notice? What if more churches had stepped up to tutor, babysit, or donate money or wireless internet hot spots? Imagine the message of love the church could have spread in that crazy pandemic time.

I started this section by challenging you to broaden your notion of who your neighbor is. Now I also challenge you to act swiftly to love your actual, physical neighbors—you know, the people who live near you. Are you connecting with them in a meaningful way that would help you to know what their needs are? Or are you merely exchanging pleasantries? This is especially vital in our social media age, an age in which we typically only see the highlight reels of each other's lives.

How truthful and transparent are we being with each other? Are we merely trying to prove we are the ones who are "put together"? In church circles there is often an added pressure of being the perfect Christian mom and wife. We are so busy showing off our chore charts, schedules, Pinterest-perfect soccer snacks, and gifts for teachers—not to mention the added pressure of proving we are frugal as we do all of those things—that I fear we, as church, are doing little to help women deal with depression, anxiety, and addiction, for example. Is that true of you? And then consider whether that neighbor you see at the bus stop or the soccer sidelines is doing well too. We all need help, and I think Jesus would want us to love each other better than we are right now.

Newsrooms and the marketplace are good at helping their employees. In fact, we have normalized the assumption that everyone needs help from time to time. When we covered the aforementioned tragedies and were running on physical and emotional fumes from serving our community, we made counselors available for staff and brought in therapy dogs. We've also organized group chats to discuss the emotional toll of significant media events like the murder of George Floyd. And if someone doesn't feel comfortable acknowledging their need for help in the workplace, we make sure everyone has the number for counseling opportunities outside the office.

The pandemic has been a particularly challenging time for everyone. Boston University's School of Public Health published a study looking at how this unprecedented time has more than tripled the prevalence of depression symptoms in the U.S., from 8.5 percent of adults before the pandemic to 27.9 percent in just the first month after many of us went into lockdown.[7] The Brookings Institute in its survey from May and June of 2020 found that one out of four women who became unemployed during the pandemic reported their job loss was due to a lack of child care.[8] This was twice the rate of men surveyed. A more recent survey shows employment among women without college degrees, who tend to experience greater occupational segregation, remains mired at 4.4 percent below its pre-pandemic

---

[7] Catherine K. Ettman, Salma M. Abdalla, and Gregory Cohen, "Prevalence of Depression Symptoms in US Adults Before and During the COVID-19 Pandemic," Boston University School of Public Health, September 2, 2020, DOI: 10.1001/jamanetworkopen.2020.19686.

[8] Alicia Sasser Modestino, "Coronavirus Child-care Crisis Will Set Women Back a Generation," *The Washington Post*, July 29, 2020, https://www. washingtonpost.com/us-policy/2020/07/29/childcare-remote-learning-women-employment/.

level—or 1.6 million fewer such women working in January 2023 than in February 2020.[9]

The pandemic also highlighted a huge gender disparity: that such events are harder on working women than on men. This presents us with an opportunity to love our female neighbors. In the newsroom we worked hard to accommodate our employees by giving them plenty of notice before asking them to return to the building after working from home during quarantine so they could make arrangements for child care. We try to do the same with schedules and planned news events, but I admit we always have room for improvement. We also work to ensure we pay men and women equitably because we know that equitable pay is right and just.

Dear church, how can we also help our women? We can help with child care, meal exchanges, or tutoring groups. And we can open up such help to everyone and avoid the possibility that these things are only done for those loyal to the "cliques" that exist within our congregations. Most of all, we can create an environment in which people can really feel safe telling others about what they need to make it day to day.

The church is supposed to be a place where the sick are healed (Mark 2:17) and where the least of these are cared for (Matthew 25). Shouldn't it also be the best place to deal with anxiety and depression? While I do believe that is the intention or desire of the church, we have room to grow when it comes to implementation. We sing "come as you are" implying that Jesus loves everyone and there is room in his kingdom for all. But all too often what we actually mean is "come find Jesus and be magically sanctified quickly so we don't have to see the unsightly fallout of your brokenness." We set unreal expectations for ourselves and others by creating spaces where we gloat—in humility, of course—about all we are already doing to demonstrate that we are perfect, instead of talking openly about how we rely on the hope

---

[9] Lily Brown, Pilar Gonalons-Pons, and Nancy Rothbard, "How Have Women in the Workforce Fared, Three Years into the Pandemic?" *Penn Today,* March 20, 2023, https://penntoday.upenn.edu/news/how-have-women-workforce-fared-three-years-pandemic.

and grace of Jesus to get by. We, the church, could certainly do a better job of being there to help people deal with both emergency and everyday stressors. If we were, then maybe the church would be the first place to which people in need would turn because it's there that they will encounter the loving care and mercy of Jesus through their neighbors—us.

Bursting Bubbles

One of the saddest things I've experienced while working in the media is how quick fellow Christians have been to make assumptions that are not true. These assumptions have been judgmental and plain mean. In fact, I cannot count the number of times I have been yelled at, written to, and addressed in an unkind tone assuming that because I am in the media I am not a Christian and cannot understand their viewpoint. This couldn't be further from the truth—*if* we are using a right interpretation of the Bible when defending those views. As a fellow believer, though I often understand their point, I've also found the Word of God being twisted and maligned to defend attitudes and perspectives that I'm certain grieve the heart of God.

The things these same Jesus-believing people have said about victims of crime or even news anchors and reporters have also been very cruel. When describing other children of God, I've heard everything from racial slurs to "I hope he rots in hell," from "Everyone in media is a tool of Satan" to "They got what they deserved." When Christians make these unloving and thoughtless comments, they tend to make them as justifications for their judgmental ideals and philosophies, which is not representative of Christ's attitude toward those in need of healing or saving. Jesus responded to adversity and the sin of man with tenderness, compassion, hope, and grace. I can only imagine that this sense of self-righteousness by judgmental Christians criticizing and spewing hatred toward others is also grievous to God, and it certainly causes the unsaved who are listening to forgo embracing a relationship with Christ. Not only is this sad to my heart, but it is also ignorant about what actually takes place in the minds of those of us who report the news happening in communities across the country. To help you understand the true ethos of newsrooms and their employees, let's look at the Society of Professional Journalists, of which I am a member.

The Society of Professional Journalists has a "Code of Ethics" that is posted in newsrooms across the country. The preamble states:

> Members of the Society of Professional Journalists believe that public enlightenment is the forerunner of justice and the foundation of democracy. Ethical journalism strives to ensure the free exchange of information that is accurate, fair and thorough. An ethical journalist acts with integrity. The Society declares these four principles as the foundation of ethical journalism and encourages their use in its practice by all people in all media.

Those four principles are: seek truth and report it, minimize harm, act independently, and be accountable and transparent. All of these principles align with scripture. From my vantage point, it's very easy to see how a journalist can be a Christian or a Christian a journalist without conflict. In fact, being a journalist has helped me become better at loving my neighbor, has broadened my vision of who my neighbor is, has habituated me to look in my own backyard to see the needs of my neighbors, and has pushed me to seek to love everyone and not just protect the folks in my own bubble. The church may have taught me the importance of these things, but the newsroom has taught me *how to do* these things.

Perhaps some of you are still skeptical. The division between church and journalism runs deep in many circles. So now may be the time for us to get this topic out of the way. When did this division between the church and journalism begin? For that I turn to what was required reading at my Christian liberal arts college: *The Prodigal Press*, written by Marvin Olansky and published in 1990 by Crossway Books. In his book, Olansky details how, in the first half of the nineteenth century, more than a hundred cities and towns had explicitly Christian newspapers. New York City alone boasted of having fifty-two magazines and newspapers that identified as Christian. This included the New York Times, which was founded by a Bible-believing Presbyterian who had a reputation for accurately reporting and exposing crime and corruption.

Olansky writes that as leading intellectuals began to attack the Christian faith, Christians turned away from the intellectual realm. They retreated into their churches and Christian schools, turning their backs on the world. Around the same time, some people began to argue that Christian publications should cover only religious topics. Existing Christian newspapers lost support. Christian journalists were harshly accused of being "worldly." And as Christians abandoned the field of journalism, they left it wide open to be dominated by people who do not share their beliefs.

I am a Christian journalist. Some Christians have described me as worldly, too. I haven't been deterred by their misguided judgment, but that attitude has kept many Christians from pursuing and engaging in journalism. The result is that there are not as many people with a Christian viewpoint as there might be making editorial decisions. While I *do not* believe the answer to this conundrum is to continue creating products, stations, newspapers, and blogs that intentionally feed consumers' desire for news that bolsters their existing viewpoints, I do believe representation matters in newsrooms. The National Association of Black Journalists, the National Association of Hispanic Journalists, and the National Association of Asian American Journalists all understand this. They are organizations that recognize that in order to ensure coverage of and stories that reflect their communities, they must have representation in newsrooms. And that representation includes minoritized people in management.

Likewise, to ensure that Christian viewpoints are in your local and national news, it is up to all of us to encourage Christians to work in newsrooms. We cannot shame young believers for going into a profession that we deem ignoble or secular, just as we cannot show the love of Jesus to the marginalized if we stay in our bubble and only work with "approved" organizations. If we only support/watch/read/listen to Fox News, or for that matter NPR or the *New York Times*, we cannot expect that we will see the entirety of the need around us.

Dear church, we have created bubbles. I burst out of mine when I defied the rhetoric that because I am a Christian—and a young woman—my gifts couldn't be found useful in a career in media. Despite hearing this from Christians, who to this day do not understand how I can be a Christian and be a journalist, doing so helped me begin to see who my neighbor really is. I'm confident now that my neighbor is not just found inside my own comfortable and familiar bubble. My eyes are opened wider, and I realize how many neighbors I have (including those on the other side of the globe).

Today I can tell you my neighbor is anyone to whom I can show mercy. This includes my physical neighbors and the people in my church family. It also includes my coworkers—those who have taught me so much about my neighbors throughout my city. It includes the victims of violence to whom I'm exposed every day in news coverage. My neighbor is also the person who just lost their home because of a hurricane or tornado. My neighbor is the kid who can't afford a backpack and whose parents can't read the English instructions to help them with their homework. And my neighbor is the person with whom I disagree on everything political and theological.

I don't know whether I would have learned of all the ways I can help my neighbor if I hadn't begun to work in a newsroom. I've learned I can be a good neighbor through my profession *and* through my church. Being a good neighbor requires that we embrace Jesus' terms and that we burst the bubbles of isolation, ignorance, and self-absorption in order to love our neighbors as ourselves.

ACTION ITEMS

1. Examine your church's outreach programs. How many are designated for your immediate community? Take a solid look at whom you are serving and what needs are being met. Is there a need not being met for which you could create a nonprofit? That would also be a way for people outside the church to see the church at work.

2. Identify who can respond fast. Because newsrooms are deadline-driven and move at lighting speed, they do very well at helping the community. Who in *your* congregation or network of people is sufficiently well connected and well spoken to respond quickly when a situation arises?

3. I understand the desire to disconnect from news and social media when times are troubling and you feel a mental break is necessary. Yet there is danger in doing so. For how do you know what's going on outside your bubble if you cut yourself off from helpful and reliable information? Another way to burst your bubble is to partner with a youth group or church in another neighborhood in your city. You can partner on projects and show up for your neighbors all over your city or town.

4. Support Christians who work in areas you may view as "secular." Representation matters. That does not mean skewing coverage to match your viewpoint. It does mean that diversity in the marketplace leads to a better world. It's crucial for us Christians to be part of conversations with people with whom we don't agree or with whom we find little common ground. If we pull back and shame Christians who work in certain areas, our Christian viewpoint will not be heard. Get Christians in the room, and be there to support them when they tell you about their challenges. Making a fellow Christian feel guilty about trying to be the light of Jesus where God has called them is not loving your neighbor.

5. Support campus ministries and colleges with programs that send Christians into the world. While not everyone is going to be a preacher or teacher and while preaching and teaching is also done through day-to-day living and working, we still have to send people outside the church walls and support them and the programs that train them—especially our young female leaders.

Self-Reflection Questions for Church Leaders

1. Why has your church chosen to support the projects and initiatives it has? When was the last time you evaluated whether those projects continue to undergird your church's mission of loving others? Is your involvement or buy-in merely out of familiarity and comfort, or is it in response to urgent need?

2. When was the last time your church led a project or initiative to reach your neighbors? When will you do so again?

3. What resources have you set aside to care for your neighbors in the event of an emergency?

4. Does your church show preference to people in certain lines of work or industries? Have those in leadership perpetuated preconceived notions that may affect how you treat the people employed in these industries in your congregation?

5. Is your church a bubble that needs to be burst? What do you need to do to burst the bubbles that exist among you?

Self-Reflection Questions for Female Leaders

1. Why have you chosen the projects and initiatives you support? Is it merely out of familiarity and comfort? If so, what needs to change?

2. Who are your neighbors? Do you know your actual next-door neighbors? When was the last time you left your neighborhood to serve others?

3. What preconceived notions may be keeping you from listening to others or serving them?

4. Are you living in bubbles that you need to burst? What can you do this week to begin bursting them?

3

Do What's Right Because It's Right

Investigative Reporters and Editors Inc. (IRE) began in 1975 to help reporters around the country share tips about reporting and writing. It still exists today. I have been a member for many years, and I have attended many of the group's conferences. A piece of IRE history I love is that a church supported IRE in its founding. At the same time, the Christian Church (Disciples of Christ) passed resolutions supporting freedom of information.[10] It also helped design the first IRE logo. You might be wondering why a denomination would support freedom of information and journalists. As we discussed earlier: because they are both about truth.

Truth is a powerful notion mentioned throughout the New Testament. John 8:32 says, "Then you will know the truth, and the truth will set you free" (NIV). Or take 2 Timothy 2:15, which reminds us to "do your best to present yourself to God as one approved, a worker who does not need to be ashamed and who correctly handles the word of truth" (NIV). Another is Ephesians 6:14: "Stand firm then, with the belt of truth buckled around your waist" (NIV).

Truth and freedom of information are aligned. If Christians believe journalists have an anti-Christian agenda, I encourage them

[10] For more study on the IRE and the Disciples of Christ underwriting, consider reading Doug Underwood, *From Yahweh to Yahoo! The Religious Roots of the Secular Press* (Champaign: University of Illinois Press, 2002) or visit GrantForward.com.

to pause and think about how closely aligned truth-seeking and freedom of information are to what we Christians believe. When you *and* journalists have access to information, *truth* can be exposed. And holding leaders accountable through truth protects your rights to religious freedom. If you want religious freedom, you must understand the importance of access to information to keep the powerful accountable.

You may flat-out disagree with what I just said, or perhaps you are still struggling to figure out how the two are connected. Organizations like IRE, the Poynter Institute, and many others focused on investigating and uncovering the truth are still around. You may have different ideas about journalists and bias in news media. But let me tell you: Christians *and* journalists want everyone to know *truth*. That's why many Christians who are journalists are passionate about their jobs. Their calling is to a purpose-filled profession, and they are committed to fulfilling it as they further the work of the kingdom.

So why is it that the majority of Christians, most of whom do not know a Christian journalist personally, find this hard to believe? I think there's a big disconnect between what they actually want from the media versus what the media considers to be its rightful job.

A study conducted after the 2020 presidential election illustrated this disconnect. It was conducted by Media Insight Project, a collaboration between the American Press Institute and the Associated Press-NORC Center for Public Affairs Research. The results demonstrated that what many Americans think of as journalism is different from what journalists consider to be their job. According to the study, 67 percent of people think it's important to be provided with the facts, but only about one in ten supports the values that drive most journalists.[11]

---

[11] Associated Press-NORC Center for Public Affairs Research and American Press Institute, "A New Way of Looking at Trust in the Media: Do Americans Share Journalism's Core Values?", April 14, 2021, https://apnorc.org/projects/a-new-way-of-looking-at-trust-in-media-do-americans-share-journalisms-core-values/.

The Associated Press commented:

> The study defines five core principles or beliefs that drive most journalists: keep watch on public officials and the powerful; amplify voices that often go unheard; society works better with information out in the open; the more facts people have, the closer they will get to the truth; and it's necessary to spotlight a community's problems to solve them.[12]

You can see these principles or beliefs echoed by glancing at the mission statements of the Society of Professional Journalists and Investigative Reporters and Editors.

Tom Rosenstiel is the executive director of the American Press Institute. He is also a former reporter for the Los Angeles Times and Newsweek. I believe he said it well when he commented on the findings on their release: "Regular people should note that when journalists say they are just doing their job, they actually mean that because they define their job a certain way. They're not lying. They really don't think of themselves as secret agents of the Democratic Party. They have th[is] set of principles that they think they're upholding."[13]

I, along with many of my Christian colleagues in the industry, resonate with Tom's point that the five values line up well with the tenets of Christianity. They demonstrate what it means to serve those in the margins. Isn't that what we're supposed to do? Isn't that what Jesus did? To help others, you must be well informed. You are not well informed if you are merely exposing yourself to the people in your own circles or bubbles.

The late Reverend Gilbert H. Caldwell, who was a journalist before going into full-time ministry, recommended:

> Rather than push back on journalists, we should ask ourselves where we would be if we weren't well-informed. If a news article makes us uncomfortable, should we condemn the messenger, or should we instead seek to understand the source

---

[12] AP-NORC, "A New Way of Looking."

[13] David Bauder, "Study Finds People Want More Than Watchdogs for Journalists," *AP News*, April 14, 2021, https://apnews.com/article/politics-media-tom-rosenstiel-journalists-915025bcab8f5910381eee11b5cb9d17.

of our discomfort? As people of the Bible, we stand for truth. Let us also stand for those who have the challenging mission of reporting the truth.[14]

I agree with Caldwell's use of the adjective "challenging" to describe the mission of reporting the truth. It's sad that some of the harshest critics of these truth-seekers are Christians. Caldwell is basically suggesting that if something you read is true but makes you uncomfortable, maybe the problem is with you and not the person who is exposing the truth.

Marshall Allen is a reporter for ProPublica, an investigative publication. In September 2018 he wrote an opinion piece for *The New York Times* called "The Biblical Guide to Reporting." In it he describes how he believes being a Christian has made him a better reporter: "The Bible endorses telling the truth, without bias. So does journalism. The Bible commands honesty and integrity. In journalism, your reputation is your main calling card with sources and readers."[15] Allen goes on to describe the parallels between journalism and what the Bible tells us to do in uncovering truth, being humble when we make mistakes, and fighting for what is right. He also writes that "most journalists admit their mistakes and run corrections. This is consistent with biblical teaching about humility."[16]

Lessons Learned about Humility

Do the right thing, all the time, even if it means you need a whole lot of humility. That's another lesson I learned in a newsroom. If you make a mistake, call it a mistake.

Whether it was due to pride or fear of legal ramifications, I once had a hard time owning my mistakes. This was evident in difficulties I had in relationships with both my peers and my bosses, and frankly also

---

[14] Gilbert H. Caldwell, "Christians Should Defend Journalists," *UM News*, October 28, 2019, https://www.umnews.org/en/news/christians-should-defend-journalists.

[15] Marshall Allen, "The Biblical Guide to Reporting," *The New York Times*, September 1, 2018, https://www.nytimes.com/2018/09/01/opinion/christianity-bible-journalism.html.

[16] Allen, "The Biblical Guide to Reporting."

on TV when I wanted to explain why we decided to report something and called it transparency or justified a decision.

This happened not only in the newsroom but in every aspect of my life, and it was taking a toll. I began to think I always had to make a quick decision. I thought people were looking to me to decide things and that if I didn't do it quickly and decisively, they would view me as indecisive or incapable of making a good decision.

At one point this became an even bigger problem in my leadership than I first realized. As part of an investment in my leadership growth, my boss, along with corporate leadership, enrolled me in several programs. One of them included what we called a "360" feedback. Basically, the company asks people above you, equal to you, and below you in the chain of command to answer a series of multiple-choice questions that rate your leadership in various areas like commanding a room, making decisions, and showing leadership under pressure. I nailed that portion. But then there were the open-ended questions. It was in those comments that I discovered others viewed me as being a "top-down" decision-maker, that I was perceived as needing to have all the answers myself, and that I was micromanaging. I was devastated. Behavior that I had understood as leading was actually deflating the very people I wanted to empower. I had believed they were looking to me for all of the answers and were loving what they heard. Instead, they regarded me as someone who thought her answers were the only correct ones and they didn't want to risk crossing me by saying "the wrong thing."

My coach, who was also a colleague, basically told me it was time for some humility and brutal honesty. You see, I had earned my position because I had proven myself as a "change agent." I thought I was doing everything I had been asked to do and doing it swiftly. I realize that I arrived at that station shortly after an ownership change, so I had expected that some of the things I had to do—like changing workflows, staffing, and expectations—not everyone was going to receive well. But most of the people who took part in the feedback exercise and made these comments about me hadn't yet understood why I was doing what I was doing. That was clearly my responsibility.

They actually liked me and wanted to please me. But I discovered that they apparently believed pleasing me was impossible.

It was clear I needed to make a change, so at a staff meeting right before we kicked off a ratings period, I decided I would address my colleagues' concerns. Traditionally those meetings had been laidback, with us enjoying food and talking about our strategy for the upcoming month. I did that. But I also explained how I had been trying to build our team for the last year. Most notably, I explained to them that I had been figuring out who could perform, who could handle the pressure, and the systems to do it. I noted that from my vantage point the team was now formed and trained and ready to fly—thus the session's theme, "The Time Is Now."

That meeting reset how the team perceived me. I could see their expressions shift as understanding dawned on them and they finally felt safe in their roles and empowered to carry the load expected of them. It was a game-changer for me as a leader—and it had been possible only because I had accepted their feedback that I needed to be humble and honest.

I'm happy to report that some of the people who were in that meeting long ago are still some of my biggest supporters and cheerleaders today. Some have even chosen to work for me when given the opportunity. Still on my desk is a clock some of them bought for me when I accepted a job in a bigger city. Engraved on the clock are the words, "The Time Is Now"—words they heard because I was willing to be show some humility.

But my lessons in humility didn't end there. At around the same time, my boss who, it turned out, did not feel as in the groove with me as I had thought, had Burkman assessments done for the two of us. One of the helpful things about a Burkman assessment is that you can have yours compared with that of a colleague, and it explains each other's stress behaviors and how you might be misinterpreting one another.

One thing that stuck out to me about my assessment was how much others misunderstood me. The feedback said: "It's important for you to know [that] Nadell doesn't really believe she is perfect. She is just devastated for you to discover that she is not."

Whoa. Yes, they were right about that. I do feel devastated when I mess up. I am not good at all at forgiving myself. I get embarrassed, and my first response is to defend my actions instead of being humble, acknowledging I'm human, forgiving myself, and moving on. And as a leader, I (and perhaps you too) am always being watched by the people who follow me. So every time I mess up and go through my unhealthy cycle of coping, all that others see are actions that do not represent the fruit of the spirit at work in me (Galatians 5:22–23). Living in the Spirit isn't the vibe I'm putting off when I lack humility!

I remember when my boss and I read that portion of the Burkman assessment. He said, "That's it! That is all I want you to do: Admit that you do not know something or that you made a mistake." Then he took it a step further, since he knew my triggers well. He told me that whenever he asks me a question, it is merely a question, not a trap or a test. It took years of us working together for me to trust that. Why so long? Probably because my reactions derived from a fear that I was wrong when everyone was looking to me to have the right answers. Nowadays I would describe that as a need to be perfect and please others. This is funny because I was doing anything *but* pleasing others; I was upsetting everyone up the ladder, my equals, and those who reported to me. Over time, however, that leader taught me to do the right thing, which for me meant learning to be vulnerable in doing so.

This brings me to an important, age-old question: Why do women—Christian women in particular—feel the need to be perfect? Barbara Minar wrote in her book *Unrealistic Expectations*:

> The bottom line is that perfectionists live in fear, fear of being their real imperfect selves. Our Lord constantly tells us to "fear not." He is not asking us to be perfect but to be in a relationship with him. He wants us to embrace our

humanness. He wants us to release our unrealistic expectation of being perfect. Only God is perfect.[17]

People often overlook this, but perfectionists tend to be hard on themselves. And this takes a toll on all their relationships. Such behavior is rooted in pride. We read in Proverbs 16:18 that pride comes before a fall. Minar explains to what pride can lead us:

1. Dishonesty—because we have to lie and live hypocritically in order to be "nice" and keep everyone happy

2. Illusion—because we have to stay in control to be perfect

3. Denial—because we cannot let ourselves know we have made mistakes

4. Defensiveness—because we cannot let others show us our mistakes[18]

To say that I have perfected humility and overcome the urge to be perfect would not be the truth. I struggle with this nearly every day. But it was in a newsroom that I became aware of it. In some instances, I have been able to be more transparent at work with my bosses than with people in my church. And I don't think I'm alone. Ladies, it's okay to be humble. It's okay to be real. It's okay to be an imperfect mom, wife, or daughter. Jesus loves you anyway.

Lessons Learned about Courage

The quest to be perfect has a strong hold in many of our heads. It did in mine. The fact of the matter was that nobody was thinking what I thought they were—namely, that I could do more than I already was. I was creating stories in my head about what people expected, and in doing so I was making fear-based assumptions. I had to learn to have courage to admit my vulnerabilities. I had to learn to have courage to include others in my thought processes and decision-making. I had to have courage to show what I viewed as a vulnerability by admitting I didn't always have the right answer and, even if I did, that I hadn't

---

[17] Barbara Minar, *Unrealistic Expectations: Capturing the Thief of a Woman's Joy* (Wheaton, IL: Victor Books, 1990), 58.

[18] Minar, *Unrealistic Expectations*, 58.

necessarily come to that answer on my own. Bringing others in shows leadership and courage, not weakness. As an admitted people-pleaser, I know this requires intentionality every day.

I learned to do a lot of this through self-reflection and emotional intelligence work. I still don't always realize immediately when I'm regressing to such behavior. But hey, at least I realize when I do it, and that's progress! I can now take the steps to ensure I catch myself *before* I act in a way that alienates others and quashes their courage.

Previous generations of leaders might have taught you that you need to be "put together" to climb to the top. Instead, I suggest you be vulnerable. Vulnerability and a perfect persona do not go together. It's when you are vulnerable that you can have courage. And to do the right thing, you must be courageous.

Brené Brown has thought and written a great deal on the subjects of courage and vulnerability. So when, in an interview on *60 Minutes*, Bill Whitaker said to Brown, "A lot of people associate vulnerability with weakness," Brown responded:

Definitely. Bad mythology. Vulnerability is not weakness. It is the only path to courage. Give me a single example of courage that does not require uncertainty, risk, or emotional exposure. No one, in 50,000 people, not a person has been able to give me an example of courage that did not include those things. There is no courage without vulnerability.[19]

Paul wrote about this in 2 Corinthians 12:9–10:

My grace is sufficient for you, for my power is made perfect in weakness. Therefore, I will boast all the more gladly about my weaknesses, so that Christ's power may rest on me. That is why for Christ's sake, I delight in weaknesses, in insults, in hardships, in persecutions, in difficulties. For when I am weak, then I am strong. (NIV)

---

[19] Bill Whitaker, "Brené Brown: The 60 Minutes Interview," *60 Minutes,* March 29, 2020, https://www.cbs.com/shows/60_minutes/video/KtGPyuGc9k6D eI_8QDbYa7acA15FCgGt/bren-brown-the-60-minutes-interview/.

When I am weak, I am strong. When I admit I do not have every answer, I am strong. When I admit I do not understand the cultural or historical backgrounds of a news story that has divided a community, I am strong. When I admit I am human and made a mistake, I am strong. When I have the courage and strength that comes from knowing I am a child of God, I can be weak, and that makes me stronger. That is when I have the courage to do the right thing. It comes from a place of weakness. And by weakness, I mean honest vulnerability.

Dear church, we must teach our young people they do not have to be perfect. Pretending to be the perfect person who has all of the answers is not who Christ called us to be. Be honest. Ask questions. Admit when you make a mistake. Have courage to do the right thing, even when people think it's crazy.

Lessons Learned about Grace and the Golden Rule

Sometimes the hardest times to do the right thing are when people seem not to deserve it. I understand the desire to punish, to set people right. But Jesus has taught me there's a better way—through grace and the golden rule.

Let's start with grace. And to do that, let's go to Merriam-Webster's definition of grace as "unmerited divine assistance given to humans for their regeneration or sanctification."[20] I didn't think much about God's grace until adulthood. Grace was rarely discussed in the Sunday school or church camp I attended. As a result, I viewed grace as something that gives people an excuse to be bad. Not understanding the gift of grace was an awful way to live. No wonder that my late teens to mid-twenties were riddled with poor decisions that made me fixate on my sin and live in misery. I didn't yet understand I could never earn God's love—that God loved me no matter what. But I was so caught up in not being good enough that I looked to attention from boys and other futile things to try to feel better. It wasn't until my late twenties when I returned to the

---

[20] *Merriam-Webster.com Dictionary*, "grace," https://www.merriam-webster.com/dictionary/grace, accessed January 30, 2022.

church that the word grace and its true meaning began to resonate with me as applicable and treasured.

In hindsight I recognize that people were constantly swarming around me to show me grace. Maybe it took rebellion to see it. Regardless, it was when I experienced grace firsthand that I finally understood how God continually extends us grace. That taught me to deal kindly with people, even when they don't deserve it, specifically in my newsroom environment. And you know what? Some Christians in newsrooms showed me that grace, too. We can't offer God's salvation to people, but we can give underserved kindness. Isn't that what we want others to do for us?

Many of you know the golden rule. Luke's Gospel, where it is found, is my favorite of the four Gospels, so let's go to the Sermon on the Mount in Luke 6:31 where the words appear: "Do to others as you would have them do to you" (NIV). This section is about loving people when they don't deserve it. Take a minute now to read verses 27 to 36.

You see, until I *understood* grace, I couldn't *give* grace. And that includes giving it to those who are my "enemies" as these verses admonish. I was so hung up on following rules and earning my way to heaven that nobody really seemed to be "good enough" in my eyes. And truth be told, I was judging them as harshly as I was judging myself. This forced me into a corner of self-sufficiency where I tried constantly to earn love and acceptance through achievement. It hadn't registered deeply enough in me that God accepts me no matter what. And while other more mature Christians bailed me out and showed me grace my entire life, it was in a newsroom that I learned how to put grace into action.

I learned that when employees crossed a line professionally in their conduct in the community or even on social media, they weren't personally attacking me by disobeying. They were often just immature themselves and making the same mistakes I had made some time before them. I learned from watching my bosses and their bosses that people often need second chances. When you support someone by being there, giving them coaching, investing in them, and showing them love, they typically thrive. They just need someone to give them that chance. And they deserve that second chance even if they take your grace for granted.

This I found one of the hardest lessons to learn. It doesn't matter if my employees are grateful. It doesn't matter if nobody appreciates steps I take to show them grace or give them a second chance. In fact, in my days of leading a newsroom, it was often the people to whom I extended the most grace or gave the most chances who were the most ungrateful. But God calls us to do the right thing anyway, no matter how others respond or fail to change after being extended grace. Galatians 6:9 sums it up: "Do not give up on doing what is right. For at the perfect time we will reap a harvest, if we don't give up" (NLT). The harvest might not happen until much later—or even while we are here on earth. But God calls us to keep doing what is right. That's how you treat people—by showing them appreciation. In negotiations. In fairness. In giving them time off. God calls us never to give up doing what's right. You might not be rewarded with popularity for doing right, which I acknowledge is a crush to the ego. But if you are a Christian and you are in leadership—and even if you're not a leader— God calls you to show grace and to follow the golden rule then entrust the outcome to God.

Lessons Learned about Making Unpopular Decisions

Another newsroom lesson I learned about doing the right thing is to make decisions for the greater good. I expect that many of you reading this think newsrooms are driven exclusively by ratings. Ratings do drive the revenue portion of our business. Naturally, the higher the ratings, the more the sales team can sell the commercials, which equals more profit.

I'll speak only for local broadcast stations as they are the only stations for which I have worked. Broadcast stations are under the auspices of the Federal Communications Commission. They are granted a license to have use of the free airwaves. To get and maintain a license, stations are required to follow strict rules, including acting in the public interest.

Acting in the public's best interest means doing the right thing, even when it makes people angry. Do you know how tough I have become by fielding irate phone calls when I interrupt a person's favorite show with a tornado warning? And yes, *hundreds* of people call complaining that their soap opera or sporting event is being trumped by lifesaving information. Luckily, weather technology has become more accurate, so we know more about the danger and don't have to cut in as often, daring to interrupt a person's favorite show to warn the public of some life-threatening danger!

Meteorologists are among the most passionate and dedicated people in our local newsrooms. I have seen meteorologists break down in tears wondering whether there was something else they could have done to save more people. Keeping your families safe is their calling. It's not a ratings or attention ploy. They are serving you, and they are glad to do it.

We know what will keep you watching TV, and we know when you tune in and out, because we receive ratings every day. We know viewers reward TV stations that do the right thing. They watch the TV stations that have a strong community presence, that give them lifesaving information, that help people in need, and that are part of their neighborhood. They also support the stations that resist the temptation to make sensational decisions—for example, by not talking to children in the heat of a tragedy simply to pull the audience's heartstrings. Instead, they remember those are children experiencing a traumatic time in their lives. They also make decisions like not showing the most sensational piece of video, the clip that shows the devastating moment at which someone learned of their loved one's passing. Such decisions are the "right" decisions.

The competitor may have earned better ratings that day by choosing to do the opposite. But in the long term the right thing is the always the best thing to do, even if you are rewarded for it only in heaven (Matthew 6:19–21).

My motives for getting into TV news weren't completely pure. Yes, I wanted to be on TV. But it was in TV newsrooms—not in church—

that I learned not to store my treasure in fame and my attention on earth. It was in TV newsrooms that I learned that decisions for the greater good were the right decisions. Jesus commands us to do the right thing, all the time. If your treasure is with him, your heart will be there, too.

ACTION ITEMS

1. Make 360 assessments available for all of your leaders. They are eye-opening. Trained coaching to address concerns and themes raised in the assessments are a great next step. If you're not a leader, ask your boss or whoever is concerned with employee development in your organization to facilitate ways for you to receive feedback from those to whom you report, those who report to you, and those who are your equals in rank. Feedback doesn't always mean compliments. Honest, anonymous feedback is not always easy to hear, but it is vital for growth.

2. There is a great need for generational training. Many of the people leading in today's workforce are Boomers or X'ers. The expectations of the people they are managing (Millennials and Z'ers) are vastly different than their own and of those who trained them. There is a great divide between the top- and bottom-of-the-ladder leaders when it comes to leadership styles and expectations in churches and in the marketplace. In the interests of successful leadership, how might you address these styles and expectations?

3. People-pleasing and perfectionism are deeply rooted in many Christian women. My journey in addressing both has come from receiving counseling and from learning to create good rhythms. How might you make mentors', women's, and teen discipleship groups and Christian counseling available to young leaders as they find their own courage and voices in leadership?

Self-Reflection Questions for Church Leaders

1. In what ways does your church or organization's mission and purpose statement reflect a culture of doing the right thing all the time?

2. How do you lead by example and encourage your leaders to demonstrate courage by expressing their vulnerabilities and bringing others into decision-making?

3. What in your organization's culture fosters an environment of humility?

4. In what ways is your church a place for people who need a second chance?

5. In conversations about news coverage involving the marginalized, ask yourself: What would Jesus' stance be on the issue? With whom can you share your thoughts?

Self-Reflection Questions for Female Leaders

1. What have you done to be a truth-seeker on behalf of the marginalized?

2. How can you help other women by being an example in showing courage through vulnerability?

3. How have you personally supported someone who showed great humility?

4. How, where, and when can you live out grace and the great commandment this week?

5. How does your personal mission statement reflect a decision to do the right thing all the time?

4

Speak the Truth in Love

Having radically candid, brutally honest, crucial, and fierce conversations is how the marketplace has embraced the biblical truth of speaking the truth in love. Jesus talked about this in his Sermon on the Mount:

> If your brother or sister sins, go and point out their fault, just between the two of you. If they listen to you, you have won them over. But if they will not listen, take one or two others along, so that "every matter may be established by the testimony of two or three witnesses." If they still refuse to listen, tell it to the church; and if they refuse to listen even to the church, treat them as you would a pagan or a tax collector (Matthew 18:15–17, NIV).

When I reflect on these verses, what comes to mind is something taught in Management 101: Talk to the person individually. Privately, not publicly. If that doesn't work, have a deeper conversation. If disciplinary action is needed, you should invite a witness to the conversation. If you go through all those steps and there is still no improvement, you may part ways. It's like an outline for how to manage people who aren't performing on their jobs. What's interesting to me is, although most organizations already have these specific steps in place to manage performance, how hard it is—both in our personal lives and in the church—to follow the words of Jesus.

Lessons about What Fuels Cruel Words

To see to what I'm referring, look at your Facebook feed or websites dedicated to spreading neighborhood news. How many posts are centered on a complaint about someone instead of following the biblical advice on how to handle conflict? How many of those complaints are written by people who consider themselves Christians? Whether it be the anonymity or the lack of personal conversations, social media has taken us down a path where we address conflict through our computers instead of in person.

I have seen the effects of this kind of cruelty in newsrooms. We have spent the past decade encouraging the people you see on TV to build their social media presence. It's a great place to reach your viewers and build a connection with them. But you can also find that it is a place where people show their nasty side. The trolls. (In the social media world, the term "trolls" refers to people who go on social media specifically to denigrate others, saying things they'd never say to a person's face.) Sadly, some of the worst things ever said to me in an email or over the phone were from people who announced they were Christians, as if that gave them a pass to speak to someone in a hateful way disguised as "righteous indignation."

Besides the anonymity afforded them to say what they please, I wondered what fuels such behavior and makes it easy to behave so badly toward others. So I did a little research. A quick Google search provided several explanations, but one in particular that has been the subject of recent conversation has to do with the lack of eye contact. The University of Haifa in Israel published a study on this subject in the *Journal of Computers in Human Behavior*. They found that the "lack of eye-contact was the chief contributor to negative effects of online disinhibition."[21] Lack of eye contact was more of an impetus for such poor behavior than anonymity.

Maybe Jesus was on to something. When we aren't looking into people's eyes to address disagreement or conflict, it's harder to see them

---

[21] Noam Lapidot-Lefler and Azy Barak, "Effects of Anonymity, Invisibility, and Lack of Eye Contact on Toxic Online Disinhibition," *Computers in Human Behavior* 28, no. 2 (March 2012): 435.

as people, harder to see the emotion they are feeling, and maybe harder to love them. And when we don't have others to hold us accountable and make sure our conversations about disagreement or correction are coming from a place of love, we may say things that aren't loving. What Jesus said in his Sermon on the Mount is far from outdated and is still applicable today.

Lessons about the Struggle—It's Real

Speaking the truth in the workplace can be difficult for many of us. In fact, the responsibility to deal with conflict directly is why some people don't pursue promotions into management positions. For those who do, it's why many fail to become successful managers. The majority of people want others to like them. They don't want to be seen as contentious or as the person who has to address all the nonsense going on in the workplace. I definitely fall into this category. Someone once described me as conflict-avoidant because by nature I'm a people pleaser and learning to speak the truth when it was something the other person didn't want to hear was difficult for me, particularly in more serious and disciplinary one-on-one conversations. I found it really hard to tell someone, "What you are doing isn't right."

So let's explore why speaking the (difficult) truth in love is difficult for so many women. To do that, I remind you of my conflict-avoidant nature. My parents will tell you I learned from masters—them. I can count on one hand the number of arguments I remember my parents having in front of me. At one time I thought that was great. Later I realized their behavior may have fostered this misguided notion that healthy people have no conflict. I heard the feedback from my bosses and coaches that I need to address problems head on. Many women find doing that to be difficult. For when a woman addresses a problem truthfully, others often interpret her to be picking a fight or not being kind. Then, if that woman tries to follow that feedback, others interpret her as not being strong enough. It's a crazy and frustrating circle.

But there is more. Many people who avoid conflict so work themselves up to the conversation that they either come off as abrasive or wait so long to have the conversation that they are not in a good mental space when they finally have it.

Strength and personality assessments are key tools in determining the source of such inclinations and behaviors. Such assessments make it easier to spot vulnerabilities, weaknesses, and strengths in yourself. One assessment tool pointed out to me that when I am stressed I'm particularly direct in my interactions—negatively so! Knowing this helps me to mitigate such unhelpful responses.

Being aware of one's emotional intelligence is critical to career success. In a study on this published in the *Journal of Vocational Behavior*, its authors found

> that emotional intelligence has a significant, positive effect on subsequent salary levels, and that this effect is: 1) mediated by having a mentor and 2) stronger at higher organizational levels than at lower levels. Our results suggest that emotional intelligence helps individuals to acquire the social capital needed to be successful in their careers.[22]

I suggest the same is true of productive personal relationships and of successful local church environments. As I climbed the ranks in newsrooms, I benefited greatly from programs that fit the above description. I never received such training and mentorship in the church because most of the programs that are similar are geared toward or available only to men. My evaluation of this situation and my experience in the marketplace prompt me to make the following three suggestions to the church:

1. *Let leading women lead potential leading women.* For women to mentor other women, you first have to empower women in leadership who can mentor. Many church programs are about how to be the "traditional good wife and mom." Where does that leave women who are wired to lead to mentor younger aspiring women leaders in the church? Many churches have long had mentoring and accountability partner programs for men. The same partnerships can

[22] Joseph C. Rode, Marne L. Arthuad-Day, and Aarti Ramaswami, "A Time-Lagged Study of Emotional Intelligence and Salary," *Journal of Vocational Behavior* 101 (May 2017): abstract, DOI: 10.1016/j.jvb.2017.05.001.

be productive for women as well. People will lean toward mentoring someone who reminds them of themselves. Dear church, without your intentional effort to include diversity in this process, it won't happen.

2. *Teach about emotional intelligence.* Instead of waiting until someone is leading in the church, we should mentor them to lead well. How? By investing in them to help them reach their God-given potential in all aspects of their lives. Whenever this happens, the kingdom benefits. Rather than waiting to have critical conversations about someone's behavior until *after* they are leading, let's intentionally grow people *into* those roles.

3. This is an area where we as the church can live out the advice Jesus gives in Matthew 18. One-on-one relationships are for mentoring. Those are the safe spaces in which heartfelt, direct conversations can happen. Don't wait for a problem to arise before entering into these kinds of conversation. Foster growth instead by normalizing and anticipating them along the way.

4. *Institute larger programs that include diverse groups of people.* If you have a discipleship group for men, launch one for women, too. In 2018 I became part of a church-led organization's first female discipleship group. It was this church's *first* all-female discipleship group. We truly lived out Matthew 18 in that group by having one-on-one conversations we didn't want to have along with some challenging conversations in the larger group setting. It wasn't always fun, but all of us are better for it.

I challenge you to create groups that include people who differ from you in race or gender. Making these in-depth connections with others is both convicting and inspiring. It was in my group that I decided to write this book! Winning for the kingdom isn't easy, but it's possible if we work together.

Lessons about Inequality in Directness

Often not addressed or even acknowledged in most circles is that many people still find it harder to have difficult conversations with women than with men. My first experience with this came from a mentor of mine in the newsroom. It was after a male manager told me to work on my "softer side." I took it to heart. That mentor of mine pointed out that feedback is hardly ever given to a man. Why is it that people often take it harder when women have direct conversations or offer feedback? People often describe such conversations as aggressive or even as a personal attack.

In 2016 professors Melissa Williams of Emory University and Larissa Tiedens of Stanford University decided to test the popular view that women are held to a higher standard of smiling more and yelling less, as Hillary Clinton's supporters argued during her presidential campaign.[23] They synthesized seventy-one studies, testing reactions to people who behave assertively. They found that women, on average, were disparaged more than men for identical assertive behaviors. Women were particularly penalized for direct, explicit forms of assertiveness, such as negotiating for a higher salary or asking a neighbor to turn down their music. Dominance that took a verbal form seemed especially tricky for women, compared with men making identical requests.[24]

Not only have I received that kind of feedback from bosses, but I've also heard it directly from female colleagues who reported to me. I once had someone in my office who recognized the discrepancy but still felt it was true and just. She admitted, "It's just harder to hear hard things from a woman. You expect a woman to be nice."

Earlier I spoke about the fact that a circle of feedback on how to behave never ends. This applies here, too. Women need support in the workplace and in the church because the struggle for understanding

---

[23] Melissa J. Williams, "The Price Women Pay for Assertiveness—and How to Minimize It," *The Wall Street Journal*, May 30, 2016, https://www.wsj.com/articles/the-price-women-leaders-pay-for-assertivenessand-how-to-minimize-it-1464660240.

[24] Williams, "The Price Women Pay for Assertiveness."

and equality is real. In fact, I believe the struggle is so significant that the frustration of feeling as if you can never win often pushes women out of leadership roles.

You may be thinking there are more women leaders than ever before. But the COVID-19 pandemic brought to light many gender disparities and the pressures on women. The National Women's Law Center tracked the statistics. It found:

> In February 2021, over 2.3 million women fewer women were in the labor force compared to February 2020. This means they are no longer working or looking for work, which brings their labor force participation level to 57.0%, a level that women have not seen since 1988, and one that has persisted for several months of this pandemic. By comparison, more than 1.8 million men have left the labor force since February 2020, and their labor force participation rate was 69.6% in February.[25]

Those statistics caught the attention of the United Nations Foundation, which suggested steps to support women in the workforce. One of those steps has to do with supporting women in leadership. The foundation made these observations and suggestions:

> Women remain markedly under-represented in senior management. Only 40 Fortune 500 companies are run by women—sadly, an all-time high—and just a handful are women of color. ... Companies should start by investing in women's advancement in the workplace with training, mentorship and professional development opportunities. Managers at all levels must be accountable for achieving gender parity, and businesses should remove gender bias in recruitment and retention practices.[26]

---

[25] Claire Ewing-Nelson and Jasmine Tucker, "A Year into the Pandemic, Women are Still Short 5.1 Million Jobs," *National Women's Law Center,* March 2021, https://nwlc.org/wp-content/uploads/2021/03/Feb-Jobs-Day-v2.pdf.

[26] Michelle Milford Morse, "Women Are Being Pushed out of the Workforce. The Private Sector Must Do More to Address This Crisis," *United Nations Foundations* (blog), March 18, 2021, https://unfoundation.org/blog/post/women-are-being-pushed-out-of-the-workforce-the-private-sector-must-do-more-to-address-this-crisis/.

Are you seeing a theme here? The marketplace understands the need for mentorship and training for advancement. The church has much to gain by recognizing this, too. After all, if women are feeling unsupported in the marketplace where the call for support is louder, how do you think women in church leadership feel, especially those who are in uncharted waters?

In the newsroom I can think of instances in which I worked hard to foster a work-life balance to maintain some incredible workers and grow them as leaders. I can think of other instances in which I could have done better, but at least I know better now. As for me, there have been times I have felt supported and other times when I have felt lonely, misunderstood, or on the verge of being pushed out. But I am more aware of the issue thanks to my leaders and training in the marketplace, not in the church.

Dear church, let's start swarming women in support. We can do this with mentorship and training. Galatians 6:2 calls us to "carry each other's burdens" (NIV). Think for a moment of how we could advance the kingdom both by carrying each other's burdens through support and training and by sending men *and* women out in the world, knowing the church will continue to support them. Imagine if we, the church, were exemplary in understanding each other's needs and in not labeling one another. Let's work harder to follow Jesus' words in his Sermon on the Mount. Maybe then we will be able to focus on loving him with our heart, soul, and mind.

Lessons about Seeing Results

The news isn't all grim: we're getting better at understanding women. And when that happens, we can speak more truth in love. Data backs this up. Since 1953, Gallup has been measuring whether people prefer male or female bosses. The year 2017 was the first in which most Americans said their bosses' gender makes no difference to them.[27]

---

[27] Megan Brenan, "Americans No Longer Prefer Male Boss to Female Boss," *Gallup*, November 16, 2017, https://news.gallup.com/poll/222425/americans-no-longer-prefer-male-boss-female-boss.aspx.

Interestingly, women were among the last to shift from preferring a male boss.

Women are tough on women, perhaps particularly when women are speaking truth, especially if it's not what the person on the other side of the conversation wants to hear. So how can a woman in leadership have the tough conversations and not be penalized for doing so? As we dive into that question, I want you to think about how these scenarios play out in the church as well and how the church is turning a blind eye to what the marketplace acknowledges is a problem.

In a *Forbes* magazine article, Dr. Shawn Andrews wrote about how women have historically failed to support each other in leadership. I'll talk about some of her points in a future chapter. In this one, I want to focus on what she described as an "invisible natural law in the female culture." As author Pat Heim coined it, the rule is the "power dead-even rule." Andrews writes:

> This rule governs relationships, power, and self-esteem. For a healthy relationship to be possible between women, the self-esteem and power of one must be, in the eyes of each woman, similar in weight to the self-esteem and power of the other. In other words, these key elements must be kept "dead even." When the power balance gets disrupted (such as a woman rising in status above other women), women may talk behind her back, ostracize her from the group, or belittle her. These behaviors are to preserve the dead-even power relationship that women have grown up with their entire lives. ... It is a big reason why women sometimes do not support other women.[28]

Wow! Andrews sums up what I have seen play out my entire life in newsrooms, personal relationships, and even the church. I have even seen women lose their jobs or be demoted over such behavior.

---

[28] Shawn Andrews, "Why Women Don't Always Support Other Women," *Forbes*, January 21, 2020, https://www.forbes.com/sites/forbescoachescouncil/2020/01/21/why-women-dont-always-support-other-women/?sh=80762363b05b.

Thankfully I've seen my workplace address it. In other cases human relations departments have stepped in when bullying amongst women has taken place.

Can you honestly say you have seen your church address similar behavior? As a woman whose job often requires speaking truth to people and who believes I should do it in love, I ask you: How are we to foster honest dialogue if we don't increase our support for the women courageous enough to have those conversations?

Lessons about Continuing to Speak the Truth in Love, Even When It's Hard

A huge part of my job as a newsroom leader was to have difficult conversations, even if the topic wasn't popular. While many of my mentors advised me always to be skeptical of people, instead I've pushed myself to give the other the benefit of the doubt and to "do everything in love" as Paul enjoins us in 1 Corinthians 16:14 (NIV).

The object of our effort to love in that verse is *everything*. That includes tough performance critiques and even cutting jobs. It includes giving people direction or feedback they may not want to hear. And those are all scenarios that play out in our churches as well.

One of the biggest compliments I've received from someone at work to whom I repeatedly had to give bad news was, "You are one of the most genuine people I know." I did make an effort to be genuine and kind no matter the message being delivered, but more than that I believe such recognition results when the people receiving the tough news from you feel heard and understood.

I've also learned that not every offense or issue reflects you, your leadership, or the culture you've created. While it's easy to take these things personally, I suggest you resist the temptation to make an issue about you and instead recognize that the person failing to perform either has some room to grow or is dealing with an ancillary issue outside of the workplace that is causing them to falter professionally. Have compassion and give grace—the same grace you are given when you need it.

In *The Complete 101 Collection: What Every Leader Needs to Know*, John Maxwell sums this up well by talking about caring for others. After all, that's what speaking the truth in love boils down to. Maxwell writes:

> Showing others that you care is not always easy. Your greatest times and fondest memories will come because of people, but so will your most difficult, hurting, and tragic times. People are your greatest assets and liabilities. The challenge is to keep caring about them, no matter what.[29]

I have had to say things the person on the other side of the table did not want to hear. People have at times stormed out of my office and slammed the door when those conversations did not go well. But I had the conversations—even when they were difficult. I learned to speak the truth—not to make myself feel better, but to help that person reach their God-given potential. That's what I mean when I say do it in love.

I know of similar conversations I should have had with people in the church. And I can think of conversations my brothers and sisters in Christ should have had with me. In Matthew 18, Jesus gives us an outline for how to address conflict. There, he also commands us to love each other and do everything in love. I learned how to carry out those commands in a newsroom. Dear church, my hope is that we, the church, will embrace more female leaders and that those women will learn how to carry out those commands in the church.

ACTION ITEMS

1. Many tools used in the marketplace to mentor employees and train them how to have tough conversations are available online. You can also find people in your church or hire someone who offers this kind of training. Use these resources.

---

[29] John C. Maxwell, *The Complete 101 Collection: What Every Leader Needs to Know* (Nashville: Thomas Nelson, 2010), 241.

2. Choose your words carefully. Ponder: How do you describe men as opposed to women around your children or teenagers? How do you describe boys and girls? In *Lean In*, Cheryl Sandberg wrote about how being described as "bossy" as a young girl affected her.[30] Pay attention to the words and adjectives you use. They make long-lasting impressions.

3. For women in leadership, partner with someone you trust and practice having these conversations. Perhaps you could also learn some breathing exercises to do before and after these conversations. Remember, until equality for women is completely attained, you will be judged more harshly than many men having the same conversation. Be aware of that fact and take steps to make sure your conversation partner feels heard and valued.

4. Many churches have accountability and mentorship groups for men. Create similar groups for women.

5. Host leadership training for young men and women in your church. Equip them with scripture-based leadership fundamentals they can both take with them into the workforce and use in your church.

Self-Reflection Questions for Church Leaders

1. What has your church done in the past and what is it doing now to grow men and women to be leaders in the marketplace and in your congregation?

2. How has your church equipped and how is it equipping men and women to carry out Jesus' advice about speaking the truth *before* they are in a leadership position?

3. How have you allowed and how do you allow people to undermine other people's leadership by not understanding insecurities that may be at play?

---

[30] Cheryl Sandberg, *Lean In: Women, Work, and the Will to Lead* (New York: Alfred A. Knopf, 2013), 317.

4. How have you supported and how do you support female leaders in your congregation when people judge them unfairly because they are women?

5. In your congregation, how do you address social media behavior that does not reflect a loving attitude?

Self-Reflection Questions for Women in Leadership

1. How have you stepped up to help other women grow in your church and in your workplace?

2. In what ways have you undermined another woman's success because of your own insecurity?

3. What triggers your stress behavior and results in you having a conversation not based in love?

4. Do you need to ask for forgiveness for something unloving you have said on social media that you would not say in person?

SECTION 2

Bridging the
Gender Divide

5

Ditch the Buckets

When I was in college in the 1990s, there were female Bible majors, but the number of female leaders teaching or administrating there were slim. I spent most of my college years seeing the girls around me scrambling to meet their husbands and graduate with their "MRS degrees" on top of their early childhood degrees. Was I failing at life and missing God's plan for me if I didn't graduate with a ring, get married, have multiple children right away, choose to stay home with them, and put that degree to work homeschooling my offspring?

Dozens of my friends and mentors have no doubt been called to that very life. I wasn't, and I definitely don't believe that's the only life God has in mind for his daughters. The problem, as I see it, was that I had no idea I had other choices as a Christian woman. I had real dreams that didn't fit the schema perpetuated by many churches, and I am convinced that God planted those dreams in my heart.

Looking back now, I recognize that the Spirit was steadily leading me to something other than these roles typically regarded as feminine. I wanted to tell stories and be part of history. A TV newsroom became the place where I could be truly me. When I was only twenty years old, my college professor made a phone call to her former coworkers asking them to hire me. A news director took a chance on hiring me as a producer and reporter though I didn't even have my degree yet. It was in that newsroom that an anchor and consultant suggested I had a gift for public speaking, writing, understanding audiences, and motivating people. They told me I could go as far as I wanted.

This was really different from my experience growing up in the church, where my destiny was limited by the highly opinionated interpretations of the apostle Paul's thoughts about gender roles. Outside of the church people spoke life into me as a young adult. They told me I didn't have limits. They valued me the way God wired me to lead.

The news station is where I used the gifts God gave me because I never felt I could fully do so in the church. I look at my early years in my career and now see a young woman who was finding her own faith and developing her own relationship with her Creator. I needed to discover God's grace and love. Until that point I had lived in fear that I was never good enough. I had been trying to find my place in this world and earn approval.

On top of that, it was challenging to encounter the questioning of my career choice. It made me question myself. When I told people I was going into radio and TV, most suggested I could work at one of the many Christian radio stations. (I did over one summer, thanks to an amazing Christian man named Gary and his wife, who gave me my first break. They were so loving, helpful, cheery, and patient, true examples of Christian mentorship.) But working at a southern gospel radio station was not what I felt called to do.

So there I was, a pastor's kid and a graduate of a Christian college, feeling aimless. Thankfully, the church exposed me to great people like my parents, their friends, teachers, professors, and people like my boss at the radio station. They were all examples who planted seeds in me. We need more of such people today.

I flourished in my job, and the investment of those people in me were part of that growth. But ultimately my opportunities to lead came in the newsroom, not in the church. Leading a newsroom includes everything from managing anchors and reporters who are household names and even legends in the news industry to negotiating financial, vendor, and talent contracts and being responsible for a multi-million-dollar budget. Here's the question I pose to you: If I had been a man, would I have been pigeonholed into cooking meals and trying to bend my gifts into the children's ministry roles? I think if you are honest, you would agree the answer is typically no. A man would have been on stage and hanging out with the senior pastor as soon as they could get him there.

You think I didn't notice that as I grew in responsibility and giftedness? I had all these talents that aligned with the talents of a senior pastor, but it was the marketplace and not the church that embraced them and me. And in the marketplace I kept growing as people kept mentoring me. It seemed as if the sky was the limit.

But at church there was a definite limit to what I was allowed to do as a woman, let alone to what I was considered gifted to do. In the marketplace I was trusted to lead people and manage the budget. That wasn't a possibility in the church because the church didn't accept all of my gifts. The church limited me to its understandings of "traditional" womanhood.

Let me be clear: I'm not saying it isn't noble to focus on your family by choosing that to be your only mission field. For those of you who have heard that calling and answered it, good for you! But that's not everyone's calling. Don't feel like a failure if God has called you to be single, to have no kids, or to work full time.

For me, God answered that question clearly. When my son was just about to turn two, my husband, Michael, and I had a conversation I'll never forget. He said, "If we're going to have another child, it needs to be now because we aren't getting any younger." My response was, "I can't believe I'm saying this, but I'm just too exhausted. I'm tired to the bone." Two months later, I found out why I had been so tired and why I had to make so many trips to the urgent care clinic for upper respiratory infections. During one of those trips, an observant doctor, who later told me she believes God often leads her to check things out, ordered a chest X-ray just to be safe. That chest X-ray showed a tumor that was later discovered to be bulky Hodgkin lymphoma. Chemotherapy cured me, but that same chemotherapy severely limited my chances of having another child.

Six years after that treatment, at the age of forty-two, I was diagnosed with breast cancer. Doctors discovered I am a BRCA2 gene mutation carrier, meaning I was at a high risk of a second breast cancer or ovarian cancer developing. At the advice of my doctor, I had a double mastectomy at forty-three and went through chemotherapy again, followed by surgery to remove my ovaries.

I was so focused on surviving for my child that it really didn't dawn on me until I was on the operating table for my oophorectomy that I wouldn't be able to have more children. As the anesthesia was starting to kick in, my surgeon gently put his hands on me to comfort me as a single tear slid down my cheek. I knew for sure God had laid out a path for me that didn't include a house full of kids.

Yes, I was sad. But I chose to answer God's calling to lead and influence others by working in a newsroom. Every time I questioned that calling, someone affirmed it again. One such encounter was with an employee who was likewise a Christian. Over dinner she asked, "Do you know how many people you have touched and influenced? And do you know how many people they now touch and influence?" Her boldly gentle reminder has stuck with me.

Ladies, you have choices. You are not a failure if God's plan for you is not what you or anyone else imagined it would be. It's God's plan for *you* and nobody else—and God is *always* good. That calling may start playing out before you realize how the "dots" in your life "connect."

Lessons Learned as a Child

Sherrie Coen cut my hair when I was a child. Her husband was an elder at the church where my dad served as the senior minister for more than twenty years, and her daughter was my piano teacher. I knew their family well. She always let me pick out a nail color and painted my nails after I got my hair cut. I liked and respected Sherrie. I remember sitting in her chair when I was ten and her saying to me, "I know everyone calls you Suzy, but I'm going to call you Suzanne. That sounds like an attorney or something professional, which I know you are going to be." I still feel excited and proud when I think of Sherrie saying those words to me.

A few years ago I saw Sherrie at my dad's seventieth birthday party. She said, "Suzy, you haven't changed a bit." I couldn't even acknowledge her compliment. I looked her in the eye and said, "You don't call me Suzy. You call me Suzanne, and you always have because you said I was going to be something. I never forgot it." She smiled and nodded in agreement. Since then, she's back to calling me Suzanne.

Sherrie made me realize I had options—which the church never did. Sherrie made me realize that even if I didn't fit into the church mold of what a Christian woman does or how she looks, God still loves me and has a plan to use my gifts.

Be like Sherrie! If you see a young woman in your church trying to use her gifts, no matter what they are, tell her you see her gifts and assure her it's okay to dream to use them. Tell her those dreams may very well be the Spirit leading her at a young age and planting a seed for her future.

These days I make it a point to share what I do with young girls and boys and for them to see me lead at church and in my community. Upper elementary-aged kids are my particular jam! I love fourth and fifth graders. They're at the age at which they still think you're cool, and they can do everything on their own. When I talk with those kids, I talk about my job. I tell them I'm the boss of the anchors and meteorologists they see on TV every day. I talk about what it's like to be at the station so they know the woman teaching them about God's grace and love through Bible stories is also a person of influence in their city. I want them to know I'm somebody who loves Jesus and prays every day that the decisions she makes helps their city and gives a voice to the voiceless. I also tell them it's fine to be a woman or man who devotes their life to raising their family. I want our boys and girls to know they have options.

During our last Sunday at our church in Pittsburgh, I spoke in the "huddle" before Sunday school classes to say goodbye to our team, and one of the moms cried while expressing her appreciation for me. She was moved that her kids got to see a strong Christian woman make it in the marketplace. The children's minister made me promise I'd keep doing what I was doing professionally and that I'd continue volunteering to teach kids that age at our new church. I did, and I kept my word.

I feel passionate about using my gifts to influence young hearts for Jesus and encourage them to grow in their passions. But I know that doesn't mean *every* businesswoman feels the same. Dear church, take the time to ask the businesswomen in your congregation how they think their gifts will best serve the body. And lest you are tempted to say, "Our greatest need is in children's ministry," ask yourself whether you would respond to a male executive the same way. Among the excellent Sunday school teachers alongside whom I have led are men who are leaders in the community. Our kids need to interact with them, too. But the bottom line is that they need to interact with both male and female leaders who are gifted to do so.

Lessons Learned about the Dangers of Buckets

You've probably heard the phrase, "You can't pour from any empty cup." It's true. We've all tried; and we all know that when we do, what comes out is a whole lot of effort with no substance. Instead of "cups," I like to think of "buckets" and to figure out what fills my employees' "buckets." Time with one's family fills some people's bucket. For others, it may be travel. For some, it's new challenges or special projects, whereas keeping to a routine fills others' buckets.

Everyone's sense of motivation is different. It's easy to assume a person's "type" and assign them to certain buckets of expectation and conditioning. When we typecast people, we rarely consider the changes they may undergo in different seasons or the boredom or disappointment they may experience when we fail to see them differently or provide different options or opinions about them, their role on the team, or what they find motivating. I find that this kind of bucket talk leads to unhelpful assumptions. It's similarly unhelpful to think we know people better than they know themselves—or even better than God knows them—particularly when it comes to gifting and personality.

After months of pushing and pushing and more pushing someone at a Tulsa TV station to be more of a leader, my boss, known as Bilte (he often goes by just his last name), said to me, "Suzanne, are you trying to teach a pig to fly?"

I had to admit I was, just as I've often believed I can transform a "C player" into an "A player." I have had to learn from failure that I can neither teach a pig to fly nor make a "C player" into an "A player."

What I can do, however, is give people a chance by equipping them with the tools for success then following up and walking the road with them. At some point, however, their journey is theirs alone. And it's up to them if they are going to use the tools I and others have given them.

What for me are some of the most helpful tools may be for others tools that pigeonhole them—like using personality assessments to determine fit and function. For me, it was when I had my first personality assessment and the person doing the assessment said, "You are often misunderstood," that I finally felt that someone understood me. When I feel understood, I grow. I have since used those tools for myself and others. Using them has reminded me I'm not an all-or-nothing person—and neither are others—just as I'm not an extrovert *or* an introvert but have qualities of each depending on the circumstance.

I've also learned I am an Enneagram 3. My StrengthsFinder strengths are Competition, Activator, Strategic, Achiever, and Maximizer. I'm an ESFP-T in Meyers-Briggs. My Burkman is a dead tie between green and blue.

Now, depending from what context and how well you know me, these results may surprise you, which is my point. I had a boss who once called me "mousy" because I was quiet around him. I was quiet around him because he was a very vocal and highly critical person. He made me feel like a failure, so I retreated. However, if you'd seen me lead a meeting back then, you'd have described me as someone fueled by people and activity. And if you know me deeply, you know I nearly always go to lunch by myself because I need to slow down and take everything in. So the key is to avoiding using such test results to typecast someone and instead to see the whole person.

These tools are helpful in determining how to manage others' stress and communication. They can also help you determine how much you really know about someone versus what you think you know about them.

I've used my employees' assessments to understand how they process things and in what environments they thrive. My manager has done the same with me. Remember the story I told earlier about when Bilte got the Birkman comparison report on me? I didn't think I was perfect, but the report revealed that I was devastated if anyone else knew I wasn't. I will never forget when my manager called me and said, "This is you! I get it now." That's what everyone wants: to be understood.

My relationship with that manager changed for the better as a result of those assessments. He's the person who taught me how to "be me" and lead. That wasn't the result of the personality work: it was me awakening to the fact that I was trying to be someone other than the real me. I finally understood that I didn't have to fit into a particular "leadership" bucket.

How can we implement such understandings in the church? When trying to empower others, don't assume someone is an extrovert because they are chipper on stage or a leader/manager because they have a spreadsheet for the supplies in the closet. One does not always mean the other. Get to know people as individuals. Use the tools available to help them assess their *true* giftings and their *real* personality.

I have been passed over for many things because people perceived me as quiet. In one case I was quiet because I was in a borderline verbally abusive situation. Someone else made assumptions about me for being too emotional without ever asking me why. If those leaders had investigated a little further rather than jumping to conclusions, I would have felt more understood, they would have understood me better, and together we would have made headway sooner.

Someone else made assumptions about me because they perceived me as talking too much in meetings. This is an area in which women are often in a double bind: we are blamed either for talking too much or for being too passive. I felt as if I couldn't win.

None of these leaders took the time to figure out why they had that perception of me. They didn't take the time to figure out what was driving my behavior. And in all those circumstances, those leaders approached me in a way that created a downward spiral of me constantly trying to prove myself. The people who led me at those times felt they knew me better than I knew myself. Unfortunately, I have done the same thing myself, and you probably have, too. We see people we want to help grow. They are loyal to us, and we see promise. We want to help them advance, but sometimes in our enthusiasm we jump to conclusions. I've had to learn that other people are not us. Their experiences are their own. God wired them in a unique way just as God wired us uniquely.

Dear church, some people are born to be leaders. Some are not. Some people may lead the way you do. Others don't. There are different, and yet still effective, ways of performing the same tasks, reaching the same goal. Nobody's way is the perfect or only way. Don't let your preconceived notions about people, success, personality types, or anything else feed your internal narrative of how someone will or should respond. Habits and the stories they have internalized have shaped them. Give them support. See if they can fly. It's up to them as much as it is to you.

ACTION ITEMS

1. Talk to boys *and* to girls about how they can take on roles in your church.

2. Look to leading men and women in your church to lead children at influential ages, but first ensure they are gifted in that area. Don't make assumptions based on gender, and don't overlook the unique way in which the Holy Spirit gifts people.

3. Get coached on how to coach. Get your leaders coached on how to coach. Don't curtail someone's growth because

you think you understand someone's motives more than you actually do.

4. Create mentorship programs. The marketplace is good at this. Mentoring pre-teen and teenage girls can open their eyes to leadership possibilities in the church and in the marketplace.

Self-Reflection Questions for Church Leaders

1. What leadership conversations are you having with teenage boys in your church—but not with girls?

2. In what ways have you hindered someone's God-given potential because you put them in the wrong bucket and made incorrect assumptions about them?

3. How do you determine the messages and lessons you share when mentoring others? Do you base them on your experiences and needs or on the experiences and needs of the person you are mentoring?

4. Whom can you tap to serve as an example for your church's boys and girls?

Self-Reflection Questions for Female Leaders

1. What steps can you take to influence young women and girls who are wired to lead?

2. What messages might be shared more frequently in your church if leaders sought the input and experiences of women?

3. Are you still living out of a bucket in which you shouldn't have been placed? What assumptions and labels have dogged you through your life? What do you need to do to climb out and come into your own?

4. Whom have you placed in the wrong bucket? What can you do to help them get out and live into their true talents?

6

Support Men Who Support Women

Real Christian men love strong Christian women. Just like Jesus did. In fact, Jesus surrounded himself with strong women. The fact that the New Testament even talks about women in Jesus' presence shows that he was radical for his day. Besides, the early church was supported by affluent women. Let's take a look at some of them.

Lessons about Strong Women in the Bible

There's Dorcas, the only woman specifically called a disciple in the Bible (Acts 9:36). Dorcas cared for others by concerning herself with the needs of the poor. Later in Acts we learn that when she died, "all the widows stood by him [Peter], crying and showing him the robes and other clothing that Dorcas had made while she was still with them" (9:39, NIV). Peter, who was moved by her testimony, raised her from the dead.[31]

I personally love Lydia. The four verses that mention Lydia tell us a great deal about her (Acts 16:13–15, 40). In those verses we learn she was a businesswoman selling purple dye and that she worshiped God. They describe her as persuasive because she convinced Paul's missionary party to go to her house. In verse 15, Luke makes it clear that Lydia is the head of her household and that Paul didn't have any problem

---

[31] Sue Poorman Richards and Lawrence O. Richards, *Women of the Bible: The Life and Times of Every Woman in the Bible* (Nashville: Thomas Nelson, 2003), 53.

with that. He baptized her and accepted her hospitality. Her home was large enough for followers to meet in it. That she wasn't married is an example of how God calls some women to be single and lead.[32]

Of the several women with the name Mary, I'm going to focus on Mary Magdalene. In Luke 8:3 we find that she, along with Joanna and Susanna, "and many others who were contributing from their own resources to support Jesus and his disciples" (NLT). Perhaps most significant about Mary Magdalene is that she was among the first to see the risen Jesus. In that it was up to them to start spreading the word, I understand Mary and those women as journalists.

In *Women of the Bible*, the authors make this point: "It's curious that if Mary Magdalene were with us today, many church pulpits would be closed to her. How wonderful that whatever hindrances to ministry may exist, no one can keep us from sharing Christ with neighbors and friends."[33] Indeed, whatever roadblocks exist, nobody can stop us from sharing Christ with neighbors and friends. That's our mission—no matter our gender. We see it in the Bible over and over again. Jesus elevated women in a time when it was more jaw-dropping than it would be today. He wanted us to see that he trusts women and views them as (capable) sisters, as does his followers. Maybe it's not what the Bible says about women that has caused so many people in the church to hold back women. Maybe it's the result of what's been said at home.

Lessons Learned about Raising Christian Boys

Before we dig into this more, I have to be completely honest: I'm no saint. I have made mistakes—a lot of mistakes. My teen years into my early twenties were filled with insecurity even though a lot of really nice Christian boys showed interest in me. The nicer they were, the more I ran. I made a story up in my head that they liked the idea that I was a PK and that they therefore thought I would be a great preacher's wife, which I was convinced I would not become. Besides, some of the "Christian" boys were straight-up jerks.

---

[32] Poorman Richards and Richards, *Women of the Bible*, 111–12.
[33] Poorman Richards and Richards, *Women of the Bible*, 126.

As an adult, I shared my story about this with a pastor's wife. She had spent years in youth ministry, and she had regularly heard high school girls raise the same concern: that the boys in their youth group were not as respectful to them as were boys who were not Christians.

As the mother of a boy, I've continued to ponder this conversation, and I've shared these reminders with some beloved friends. While I was rambling on about how the church has failed in this area, a fellow "boy mom" spoke up and said, "This starts at home."

How true. What are our boys seeing at home? How are we treating each other at home? How are we talking about strong women in our homes and in our Sunday school classes? What image of women are we planting in our boys' minds? I'm not going to get in the debate about specific gender roles. But let's remember that Jesus himself often showed women particular respect, as it were giving women a seat at the table. They were his friends (Mary and Martha). They supported him (Mary Magdalene, Susanna, Joanna, and Dorcas). His longest one-on-one conversation recorded in the Bible is with a woman (the woman at the well). And when he wanted to spread the news that death would not defeat him, he chose women as the messenger to do so.

Our boys need to know that respect in a relationship is earned, not granted because of their gender. Far too few of our boys in the church are getting that message. It is up to us to stop the locker room mentality often found in Christian homes that demands a self-centered respect toward the male head of the home and believing that means weakening the wife. Saying a wife is strong does not mean the husband is weak.

I'm the chief breadwinner of our family. I've also been the spiritual leader in our house. That doesn't in the least belittle Michael or his faith. In fact, I'd argue Michael is stronger than me in many ways. He holds our household together. He deals with snarky comments from other men and women about being the parent who does most of the caregiving for our son. The strength we have as a couple is founded in Christ and in our mutual acknowledgment of each other's strengths. At the end of the day, I believe the nature of our health and stability comes down to that. It's not that one of us is stronger than the other: we're just different. And we don't approach our lives with a square peg/round hole mentality just to fit what other people think we should do or be.

By the way, I think that makes my husband so much more attractive than any man who diminished me to elevate himself.

This concept of playing to our strengths is well illustrated in the Bible. Among the early church's biggest supporters were Priscilla and Aquila. In *Women of the Bible*, the authors suggest the fact that "Priscilla is named first in three passages and Aquila is also named first in three indicates that these two were truly equal partners. Neither was the leader; neither was the follower."[34] Women, that means that when you are elevated, you do *not* turn around and diminish your spouse.

I believe that if Jesus had not wanted women to be elevated, the apostles would have omitted the story of these women from the collection of texts that became the New Testament. There were plenty of men about whom they could write. But the Spirit led them to write about Priscilla and Aquila. And while I think it's important for men to hear this message, it's equally important for women to hear it, for many Christian women who are gifted to lead feel guilty or that they are not being good Christian wives if they use their God-given gifts.

If you are not a woman who is wired to lead, how do you talk about women who are and who are using those gifts in "untraditional" ways? Many women in this position have spoken of having a range of emotions in response to other leading ladies, including jealousy, disdain, confusion, and indignation. Are any of those feelings seeping out in the words you speak in your home? You know the saying, "Watch what you say when little ears are listening." How do *you* describe women leaders? How do you describe married couples in which the wife has a more elevated or public or prominent role than her husband outside the home? Do you lift others up? Or do you criticize them because they make you feel insecure or simply because they are called to a different kingdom-furthering path than yours? The messages you deliver at home are just as important as those delivered from the pulpit.

---

[34] Poorman Richards and Richards, *Women of the Bible*, 161.

Lessons Learned the Hard Way

I don't remember ever hearing Priscilla and Aquila described as a "power couple" in spreading God's word, not in the way I have heard people talk of Paul and Silas and Barnabas. This is interesting to me because in some ways the home in which I grew up was not a particularly traditional Christian home. Yes, I was a small-town PK who grew up in a church where women were not even allowed to serve communion. And yes, if asked, my parents would describe themselves as complementarian and say it is the man's job to be the provider, both materially and spiritually. Nonetheless, I knew my mom's career was an important support to our family. She was the breadwinner and went back to school to further her career when I was in elementary school. The conflict in my mind arose as I became older and more aware. My mom still fit the expectations of traditionalists because of her "traditionally female" career as a nurse and because, to my knowledge, she never pushed to lead in the church.

As I grew older and became more aware of my gifts, it was clear that my choices to lead would not be entertained in church. Even though I couldn't use them *fully* for the Lord in the church, I knew I'd find a way to use them somewhere else.

Likewise, I certainly wasn't going to marry a boy from my home church or Christian college because they'd probably just hold me back. Instead, in my mid-twenties I fell in love with an agnostic graphic artist. He was eight years older than me, and he was nothing like anyone I had dated before. But somehow, I knew it would work— well, kind of.

Before Michael and I started dating, I vividly remember telling my mom that this guy at work was going to ask me out and that if I agreed I knew I'd be engaged to him by the end of the year. The only reason that story doesn't sound creepy is that it's exactly what happened.

My path is not one I would recommend. My first decade of marriage to Michael was rough. I fell in love with him and we were married during a period in which, though I still described myself as a believer, I was not involved in or even attending church. I had hit bottom financially and emotionally. My parents, who had extended me so much grace, were exhausted by me.

When Michael and I became engaged, I lied to my dad about going to pre-marital counseling because I knew any counselor would advise us not to get married. What followed were years of marriage counseling and some heartache. I knew I was unequally yoked, and we came awfully close to divorcing several times. I'm happy to say there was a favorable outcome to the mistakes I made.

When Michael entered my life, he was nothing like the boys I usually chased. There was something different about him. I was drawn to him because he challenged me. He didn't hold his intelligence over me, but he did challenge me. He was old-fashioned and nice. He hunted me down before I headed home that Christmas to wish me a good holiday. And when he asked me out on our first date, he did it by asking me if he could walk me to my car when my newscast was over. What hooked me was that there was never any power struggle between us. We never looked at anything as *my* job or *your* job. He's an artist, so he's had as much say in decorating our home as I have. He cooks. He has been our son's primary caregiver. We've shared and handed off the financial books to one another at different times. Yard work we have shared between the two of us in whatever way we can. We just get it done.

I'm not sure when we decided I would be the one to deal with company politics and climb the ladder first while his career took the back seat. I don't know if he just decided to take the back seat because he knew my gifts. All I know is I wouldn't have been able to influence and advance the kingdom in the ways I have if Michael hadn't regarded me as someone whose gifts were given by God and needed to be used. And he figured that out while he was still figuring out his faith. That's much more than many boys realized who'd grown up in the church.

Nowadays we do kingdom work together. After being married for fourteen years, Michael heard a sermon at my home church about being "all in" and not waiting until it was too late. In the two years prior, Michael had been with me during my first cancer battle, one of his closest friends had died of ALS, and his dad had died suddenly of a heart attack. After that sermon, Michael decided to be "all in" in our marriage and in his faith. People who had been praying for him and us for years rejoiced. The church to which we belonged in Oklahoma partnered him with someone who taught him the basics of the Bible and helped him grow in faith. Ever since, Michael has played drums in worship bands in the cities where we've lived. If there is a church food train, he signs up and cooks for whoever has a need. And he fully supports me in whatever ways I'm called to lead.

I honestly don't know where we'd be today if Michael hadn't taken that leap of faith. And while I now see how God has been with us along our winding, bumpy relationship road, I don't want other young women to feel they must travel a similar path to be supported.

Let our kids see the Priscillas and Aquilas! Let our kids hear us speak about them in ways that honor how God has gifted each person (man and woman) differently! Let our kids see it's an act of worship when people use those gifts and when we honor their use of those gifts! Let our kids see that we can elevate others without belittling ourselves!

Lessons Learned from Business Leaders

Besides in our home, I have also felt empowered by men at my workplace. I have had some extraordinary male bosses who helped me learn how to lead by embracing my God-given talents. They never expected me to be someone else; they simply helped me be the best version of me.

I've talked previously about Bilte, the VP/general manager at the station at which I worked in Tulsa, Oklahoma. We were an arranged work marriage. We were both dropped into the station sight unseen after our company purchased the station for new roles and opportunities for us both.

Before I met him, he was described to me as being "salt of the earth"— a good man. It was true. He was raised Catholic but would go out of his way to tell you he isn't religious. But he was good to people—all people. Even if he was on your case, you knew it was because he wanted you to succeed.

The first time I felt fully trusted as a female leader was thanks to him. I know I'm the leader I am today because I worked with Bilte. And I'm not the only female leader who would tell you that. I once asked him why that was. He simply said, "I just treat everyone the same." And you know what? He does. He didn't have special "guys' club" dinners or hangouts. He invited us *all* to *everything*.

I know there were times I probably went too far, but he reeled me in and let me keep leading and finding my way. When I was losing patience in bringing my managers along, he coached me to meet them where they were. When I needed to pause and find ways to thank people and make them feel good to keep them motivated, he'd step in and make sure we were getting that done. Bilte let me have the spotlight when he knew it would help me grow. He knew that doing so wouldn't diminish him. He knew we were better when we were both strong.

In some ways I find it sad that the first leader who really elevated and honored me for me would not describe himself as spiritual. Moreover, my choice of spouse was rooted in the fact that a man who was not a Christian at the time treated me better than any self-described Christian man I had dated before. This told me that I was finding more validation for my strengths and gifts outside the church than inside.

My hope and prayers are that young women in the church don't have to go searching outside their faith to find that kind of appreciation and empowerment. Girls, look for boys whose parents have raised them to be secure enough that they are not threatened by a girl who is gifted to lead. I promise they are out there.

Remember, too, that your gifts are God-given. Find your church and find your people. Don't get frustrated and think there is nowhere in the church for you. Women were a key part of the early church. You can still find a place to use your leadership gifts today because it's still a living expression of the body Jesus loves. And he loves *all* of it.

ACTION ITEMS

1. Expose our boys to Christian women who are leaders. (This assumes we have previously shown our girls they have choices and have mentored them into leadership roles.)

2. Watch what you say at home. Watch what you say about other people's lives. Remember that children may be listening.

3. Explore what you really believe about gender roles in marriage, work, and the church. There are great books about what the Bible really says. Do you believe what you believe because of what you know or because of what your ears heard when you were little? You can also speak with your pastor about gender roles and read books. Some suggestions for the latter include Sue Poorman Richards and Lawrence O. Richards' *Women of the Bible: The Life and Times of Every Woman in the Bible*, Ron Highfield's *Four Views on Women and Church Leadership*, Scott McKnight's *The Blue Parakeet*, and Kadie Cole's *Developing Female Leaders*.

4. Do what you can to make Christian counseling easily available to your congregation. We often make poor decisions, especially in early adulthood, because we imagine others' expectations. Young adults may need to talk through things with someone and know they can do so in confidence. There are many non-Christian voices in the marketplace, bookstores, and social media. Some of them are wise, but we do well to make Christian voices available for our young men and women to hear and consider, too.

5. Don't judge. God's not finished with you or your family. Focus your attention on your own and your family's calling instead of someone else's.

Self-Reflection Questions for Church Leaders

1. How much time have you spent focusing on the women of the Bible in your sermons and discipleship classes? What about in kids' and young adult programs?

2. What messages are you are giving to men and women in your church about their roles? Does your messaging infer that elevating one's own role means diminishing another person's role?

3. How do you support the Priscilla and Aquila couples in your church?

4. What steps do you take to support someone in your church who is in an unequally yoked situation?

5. How do your leaders lead by example by sharing the spotlight to elevate both men and women?

Self-Reflection Questions for Female Leaders

1. When have you spent time studying women of the Bible and the examples they set?

2. How do you talk about other women, especially women in leadership, around others, especially children?

3. If you are in an unequally yoked situation, what steps are you taking to ensure that your faith is growing nonetheless?

4. If someone is elevating you, how are you making sure you are not diminishing them?

7

Shake Your Double Standards

Some of my most critical lessons learned have been through hearing some tough words. On more than one occasion, I have heard colleagues talking about how hard it is to manage the double standards set for them as working women, even when they may be unconsciously imposed.

One such discussion centers around being expected to manage their careers and their homes in ways rarely expected of breadwinning men. Some men don't fully acknowledge that their wives keep their family's life together and that, by doing so, they make it much easier for the husband to concentrate on work. The women infer that they are probably also taking care of additional matters at home.

During a work move from one city to another, I was talking to a woman who had once owned television stations. I was explaining how hard it was to focus at work while my husband juggled looking for a job and getting us settled in the house. I then shared my frustration that my boss at the time had commented how surprising it was that we were not yet settled in our home. My friend replied, "He doesn't understand because his wife was at home taking care of everything so he could focus on work." It was true.

Another female leader in my company shared that once, during such a relocation, she and her husband were fine with him taking the lead on getting their kids settled in school so she could focus on work during work hours. Nonetheless, a school administrator reached out to her for every question the school had about the kids; and, when corrected that school administrator commented that the school wasn't used to reaching out to fathers.

The stigma around "boys clubs" runs deep. I'm referring to how the mood shifts in the room the moment a woman walks in. It's as if she stopped the conversation in its tracks. And she probably did walk in on an inappropriate conversation. Men, you need to know this. It is often very obvious to a woman in business when she is the only woman in the room or on a trip. You don't need to point it out to her: you just need to treat her with respect. That includes the nature of the conversations you have with other men when a woman isn't around—or, better yet, don't have those conversations at all.

Likewise, most people would never talk to a man about his need to show his softer side, to be less opinionated, or not to appear too aggressive. Meanwhile, many women in leadership receive such unfair criticism daily.

A suggestion from an employee to my boss that I was too intense was passed on to me. It stung for a second, but I knew that both the employee and my boss had good intentions. And let's be honest: I *am* a bit intense. The point is that men typically do not have to worry about striking the perfect balance between being too emotional, too aggressive, and not too passive. Nor do men typically have to worry about expressing their opinions. For women, it's exhausting!

Some people don't understand how unfair it is to be given a higher salary or bonuses simply because they are the chief breadwinner of the family or they have kids in college. Or how awful it sounds to a woman to hear someone say, "Losing this job has to be so hard on him. He was the breadwinner, you know." Seriously. I'm the breadwinner. And my son will hopefully go to college someday. And any female chief may be in the same boat. And even if her husband also earns a good salary, why should she get less of a bonus because her husband chose to work and her male counterpart's wife chose not to? Shouldn't pay be based solely on merit or value that a person brings to a job?

Men being aggressive in a situation or with another employee has been accepted behavior for centuries. But in the 2020s, if women behave the same way, we openly refer to them as a pack (as if women were barking dogs!). If you are someone who refers to women in this way, I implore you to think about what you are saying. How you express yourself signals how you view women in the workplace.

Some people don't understand why it shows bias when they say, "We have a new boss, and she's a woman." To point out that your new boss is a woman typically implies that you expected your leader to be a man. It also implies you may expect different behavior from that leader because of her gender. In spite of findings that more and more people do not care whether their boss is male or female, to some people it apparently still matters, even if they don't say so out loud.

Women are graded on everything from what they wear to how they do their hair and whether their nails look neat and feminine. We have conditioned women to believe spending money on those things is required to climb the leadership ladder and that they will be judged on their appearance. Are men sent to "executive presence" training and assessed on whether they are over-dressed, under-dressed, too masculine, or too feminine in appearance? The default executive option for men may simply be a suit. For women, pantsuits, skirts, blouses, dresses, hair, and makeup are all assessed—and typically found wanting in some regard.

Some people don't understand why it's wrong to be upset when a female boss doesn't do something nurturing, particularly when they would never be upset if a male boss didn't do it. A male employee once asked whether I didn't like the newsroom staff because I didn't cook for them as much as I had cooked for my previous newsroom. Indeed, I didn't cook for that newsroom as much—because I was swamped with both personal and work issues, not because I was being neglectful or showing favoritism to one staff over another. I'm fairly confident the employee would not have asked that question if I were a man. He wouldn't have expected a male boss to spend his spare time baking for the team.

Some people may never understand the pressures on a woman leading in a world of double standards. All the above examples happened to me or I personally witnessed them, and they all hurt. Those words were painful to hear when I had worked so hard to be treated equally, and sometimes I had to work hard to keep my emotions in check. In each case, it was the women in my workplace who helped me by letting me vent or by giving me sound advice.

But on some occasions the women with whom I have worked have exacerbated these stigmas and biases by supporting the same unfair expectations of women in leadership. I mentioned in chapter 4 an article in *Forbes* in which Dr. Shawn Andrews identifies reasons women don't often help each other in the workplace. She writes:

> Because of obstacles women face in their career and corporate environments, and the achievement of hard-fought success, their attitude toward other women is "I figured it out, you should too." Executive women are often overly encumbered with daily duties and responsibilities and don't take time to mentor and support young women.[35]

I wish I could say I was always helpful. Unfortunately, I too told other women, "You'll figure it out." Why? Simply because I was often overwhelmed myself. But you know what? I can help to stop these perceptions and the cycle of poor treatment and start supporting other women more. We all can.

As Christians, God calls us to do more to help and love each other. God calls us to go the extra mile. Each situation discussed so far is not only a double standard but also a direct opposition to a mandate of scripture: God's desire for his children to live in harmony with one another (Romans 15:5–7).

Dear church, let's get back to regarding each other as Christ regards us—as brothers and sisters. When we do that well, we praise God. When we prefer others over ourselves, we praise God. Let's do what Romans 12:10 enjoins us to do and "be devoted to one another in love [and] honor one another above ... yourselves" (NIV).

---

[35] Andrews, "Why Women Don't."

Such devotion and honor pay attention not to outward appearances but instead to our essential being (1 Samuel 16:7, 1 Peter 3:3–4). Second Corinthians 10:7 aptly sums up the differences between the two, reminding us that "You are judging by appearances." Instead, "If anyone is confident that they belong to Christ, they should consider again that we belong to Christ just as much as they do" (NIV).

When I caught myself not living out these biblical commands, what helped me get out of the rut was praying for the people I was judging and reminding myself daily in my journal that "we are all children of God." I found that when I look at each person I encounter as a child of God, my heart softens and they begin to look different to me. You will, too. You will find yourself wanting to help and wanting to give others the benefit of the doubt rather than judging them. With time, you will recognize that their situation isn't fair. You will recognize, perhaps, that you weren't held to the same high standard as them or that their situation is a hard one. It's when we look at each other through that lens of mutual recognition, compassion, and thoughtfulness that we offend others less and offer to help them more.

Lessons Learned about the Prevalence of Double Standards

Offending less and helping more is all about diminishing these double standards. What has helped me acknowledge then work through the double standards I was experiencing in the marketplace was learning that my sisters in Christ deal with the same thing in the church world then receiving their hard-won advice.

One area in which most male church leaders have not made much progress is in what they allow (let alone encourage) women to do. Their denomination may be permitting women to do more in leadership, but is that denomination encouraging and pursuing women to lead as much as they pursue and encourage men to do so? Jen Wilkin, the author of *Women of the Word*, wrote about this in her blog.

1. It is one thing to say women are permitted to be deacons, and quite another to actively seek out and install women in that role.

2. It is one thing to say women are permitted to pray in the assembly or give announcements, and quite another to ensure that they are given a voice on the platform.

3. It is one thing to say that women are permitted to teach women, and quite another to deliberately cultivate and celebrate their teaching gifts.[36]

I might add: It is one thing to permit women to preach and quite another to engage her sermon rather than assess how she looked in the pulpit.

Do we comment on a man's hair or clothing or friendliness in the pulpit? Rarely.

No wonder that when women hear these complaints, they feel as if they can't win. And I'm sure that the men who are awesome enough to support them feel exhausted by these shallow criticisms, too.

Let's face the reality: Double standards exist for women in most areas of employment and service, whether in regard to compensation, appearance, expectations, achievements, or manner. In some ways we are doing better at this as a society, but there is more to be done—and this is especially true of how we treat women in the church. Dear church, let's work together to make it better for the next generation.

Lessons Learned that Can Help the Next Generation

To the women reading this: Don't get discouraged. Hang in there. I truly believe we are making progress. While I spent the first part of this chapter sharing examples of how men and women generally are not helping women, there are exceptions. Some people do actively help other women. Others who aren't quite there yet need someone like you to point out that what they were saying or doing is hurtful and destructive and that God calls us to do much better than that.

Thankfully, I now see more male leaders pointing out inequity in pay and taking steps to resolve it. They are reading books and engaging in hard but meaningful conversations to understand and remedy the

---

[36] Jen Wilkin, "The Complementarian Woman: Permitted or Pursued?" *Jen Wilkin* (blog), April 23, 2013, https://www.jenwilkin.net/blog/2013/04/the-complementarian-woman-permitted-or.html.

problems that men have historically caused, perpetuated, excused, and overlooked. And they are going the extra mile to ensure there is diversity at the table. This is a good time to be a woman!

Seeing women helping each other in the workplace has motivated me to do so, too. If you have felt alone, then be the mentor you wanted. And if you have had amazing mentors, then pay it forward. It's up to us to pull that colleague aside and show her how to respond to the male leaders in the room in order to get a quick win. That same leader, more than once, has motioned for me literally to "sit at the table." When I resisted because my presence seemed to make the men uncomfortable, she said, "No, stay." That leader and two others on our executive leadership team did that or something similar repeatedly. In doing so, they were making a statement: Sure, they wanted me to be heard and seen. More than that, they were signaling to everyone in the room that the old rules no longer held and that it was everyone's task to empower another woman to step up.

This takes time. At one meeting I recall passing on an opportunity to have a seat at the table, fearing I'd be overstepping my bounds. Later another female executive pulled me aside and told me never again to relinquish such power and opportunity. She taught me that when we women show up, it teaches men that their patriarchal rules no longer apply.

The same principles apply in the church. I thank God daily for a group of women I met in a discipleship group, whom I'll describe in more detail later. You know what I love about these women? That we don't let our insecurities get in the way of helping each other.

Unfortunately, I don't have deep experience of women on different paths who support one another unequivocally. In my career, the less I was able to participate in events, groups, or studies during times more convenient for stay-at-home moms, the less I could do this in the church, too.

Inevitably, this lack of contact and communal influence in my life created an emotional divide between me and other women. I didn't feel included, understood, or supported. Other women said things like, "I'm fortunate my husband is a good provider so I don't have to work," or, "It must be so difficult for you to be away from your child so much; I just don't know how you do it," or, "I put my kids over my career; I don't know how a good mom could do anything else." The more they did this, the more different and lonely I felt.

What thoughtless and unkind words! Dear sisters in Christ, please remember that many Christian women work because they believe God has called them to their profession—and/or because of economic necessity. It has nothing to do with their husband's lack of ability to provide or the women's lack of love for their children. In my particular situation, Michael's career path would have supported us just fine. And honestly, I believe that, given my personality and calling, I've been a better mom to Price as a working mom than if I'd stayed home. This is simply the way I feel God designed and purposed our family.

Dear church, let's stop looking at our differences and letting our insecurities associated with those differences get in the way of leading others toward positive change. Let's bring each other along and recognize that God intends something different for each person and each family. When we are offered help or perspective, let's receive it graciously and pray for that person's well-being.

As for the men and women who don't yet understand why this is such a big deal, I challenge you to look around and ask yourself: How would I have wanted my younger self and her Spirit-led hopes and dreams be nurtured to fruition? How would I want this for my daughter or niece, aunt, or mother?

ACTION ITEMS

1. Review how your staff and leaders are being trained, and ensure that they understand the history of discrimination and gender bias in the workplace, churches, and culture in general. An outside facilitator might help you with this. The marketplace has many materials on the topic available for managers, leaders, and staff—including of churches.

2. Evaluate the pay of the men versus women on staff. Is it fair? If not, now that you know, what will you do about it?

3. Evaluate your policies. What policies do you have regulating women in leadership that you don't have for men? With that knowledge, what will you now do to erase such discrimination?

4. Examine the discipleship programs available in your church as well as in your small groups. Do they show preference for couples and people who have similar paths? Ensure there are options for men and women, and prevent cliques from being formed by deliberately making opportunities open to everyone.

5. If you have a (young) woman on your staff or in leadership and there is not a female mentor on staff, find one for her. This mentor can be someone from another congregation or organization. Find someone to coach her and talk with her about how to thrive in your church.

Self-Reflection Questions for Church Leaders

1. Have you offended a female (leader) when you thought you were helping? What, if anything, did you do to explore why she felt offended? What can you do now to make things right?

2. What steps have you taken to understand gender bias in the workplace and culture?

3. When have you favored pay or benefits to male leaders over female leaders by assuming they were the chief breadwinner in their household? What can you do now to make things right for them and for others in the future?

4. What kinds of programs and groups do you have available to people and families in your congregation who aren't part of the "traditional" Christian family mold?

Self-Reflection Questions for Female Leaders

1. If you don't have a strong mentor, to whom might you reach out? You might have to be the one to initiate such a relationship.

2. Have you spoken to someone who has repeatedly offended you? If so, what did you say to help them understand?

3. What have you done to advocate for women or others who are not treated equitably in the workplace or in your church?

4. What have you done in terms of establishing groups, mentoring, or studies to help lead the way in your congregation so everyone has opportunities to participate and grow?

8

Listen First, Speak Later

"The next time you are in a meeting, I want you to do something before you speak up. I want you to imagine yourself picking up a glass of good wine, taking a slow sip, enjoying the taste, and then setting the glass down. Do that before you say something." That is one of the best pieces of advice I have ever received from Bilte.

As you know by now, Bilte taught me a great deal, including how to appreciate a good glass of wine, which is why I think he was proud to use that example. He told me afterward that he had once received the same piece of advice, except the illustration was to imagine smoking a good cigar. He knew I wouldn't appreciate that example one bit, but a good glass of wine? Yes, I could identify with that just fine!

Lessons Learned about Listening More

Indeed, I needed to slow down to think and listen before I spoke. I had a tendency to blurt out whatever I was thinking in the moment rather than pause to consider how my thoughts would affect those hearing them. Granted, it's a trait that has served me well in many instances. It has helped me to keep meetings moving along and to drive critical conversations and thought. That's vital in news editorial discussions and in leading any group of leaders. I can make a quick decision, act on it, and articulate what I want; and that capacity has served me well first in producing newscasts, then in managing newsroom teams, and finally in managing an entire team. But overall it has landed me in more trouble than it has avoided, and it has alienated more people than it has united. This was a problem long before I admitted it. I spent so much time in my early leadership days focusing on trying to make everyone happy and defending my behavior that I didn't hear their advice to listen. I would have saved myself a great deal of frustration and tears if I hadn't been so much wanted to be seen as the person with the answer, and instead as the person who bothered to listen. Bilte made this a bold priority when he managed and mentored me. And I finally heard him loud and clear.

As I look back on my career, I realize much of the advice I've been given has concerned listening more and speaking less. I've learned you can't hear others if you constantly interrupt them with comments—or even commands—that at times appear frantic. And you know what else? Others won't hear you. They'll merely notice that you're too intent on being heard to listen to them.

Marian, a woman for whom I worked for over twenty years, once suggested that I put a rubberband on my wrist or move a ring to the other hand as a reminder to slow down when I'm in high-pressure situations. Later in my career in that same newsroom I happened upon my old personnel file and in it a plan Marian had put together to help me focus more on leading from my strengths. But it also listed as my main weakness my unwillingness to listen to my colleagues and my tendency to rush to decisions. Marian also invested time in helping me to capitalize on my strengths made her accurate criticisms of me easier to take on board.

If you are a believer, you know this dynamic is an example of living out James 1:19: "My dear brothers and sisters, take note of this: Everyone should be quick to listen, slow to speak and slow to become angry" (NIV). With years of practice I've found that I'm slower to become angry if I stop and listen, if I pause to take a few slow sips of that imaginary wine.

The fact that James addressed both the "brothers and sisters" in this verse is interesting to me. Perhaps it was merely a convention. But perhaps he wanted to make sure people of *both* genders were listening. I wonder: In those times, was the "he said/she said" debate on who was a better listener already an issue? We're wired differently, and that can create conflict when it appears that we're not listening to each other.

Kadi Cole writes about this in her book *Developing Female Leaders*. She notes: "Men tend to interrupt to gain control over the dialogue or to turn the conversation in a specific direction. Women, on the other hand, tend to interrupt to create connection and confirm understanding."[37] Understanding those differences is key to raising up both male and female leaders. It's also key in understanding how others see you and why you may not be perceived as a good listener.

Seventeen-plus years into holding a manager title, I am still working on this. The pandemic forced me to improve. There is nothing like a remote (Zoom or Teams) meeting to bring home how much we talk over each other. This format makes it far more obvious how often I jump over others to get my point across before the moment is lost, and how I then end up apologizing and feeling embarrassed. As my awareness of doing so has increased, I've learned to click that golden hand icon during virtual meetings. That helped some. But I needed to do more. So I asked myself: Why do so many leaders struggle with this?

I realized that what drove my rudeness and lack of respect for others was a desire to prove I deserved to be in my position. I was constantly trying to demonstrate I wasn't weak and that I had The Answer. It's as if I was screaming, "Look at me, I have the answer! Look at me, I can solve your problem! Look at me, I really deserve to be here!" Who wants to be around such a person? No one.

That's an ugly realization. In my journey of self-awareness and emotional intelligence I worked really hard not to appear as someone who was arrogant, someone who was convinced she had all the answers and didn't want to hear anyone else. Though I wanted to foster an inclusive atmosphere, my actions didn't demonstrate this desire. Part of my journey to greater self-awareness was realizing people are often skeptical of giving their thoughts and opinions when the boss is around, even when the boss says it's okay to do so. Whether that is the result of a long-standing cultural practice or the result of experiencing

---

[37] Emily Cole, *Developing Female Leaders: Navigate the Minefields and Release the Potential of Women in Your Church* (Nashville: Thomas Nelson, 2019), 74.

bosses who were less open to input than they claimed, the fact is that it can be hard for employees to speak up.

I knew I didn't have all the answers. So what was prompting my insistent behavior? Being enmeshed in a hierarchical culture, one in which direction and strategy came from above and those below were expected to execute their bosses' decisions. I thrived in that culture because I took direction very well.

But as I became a leader myself, I questioned whether people actually saw me as the boss—or as an imposter. Soon, to feed my insecurities and emulate what I had experienced for so long, I slipped into believing I was the one with all of the answers—the correct answers.

Why was I behaving this way? Because I'm wired to be an achiever and I often base my worth on achievement. Because knowing that people recognized the worth of my suggestions was a form of achievement for me. Because knowing I'm making a difference in the world through such achievements fuels me. But was I using those achievements and the means to those achievements for good? Or were my insistence and verbosity, and my drive to prove myself, harming others by silencing them?

What have I learned from this? That it's useful to figure out why a female leader is either silent or verbose. Now I ask myself: Does she feel incompetent or unworthy? Of what or of whom is she afraid? Or is she verbose because she has a good solution and is offering it to the team? A person operates at her best when she feels heard.

God enjoins us to be quick to listen, slow to speak, and slow to anger. I find that challenging. Years after my epiphany about my own tendency to dominate, I'm still working on this one. It's worth the effort.

Learning from My Helper

The voices to which we listen matter. The most important among them is the voice of the Holy Spirit. I didn't grow up in a home or a church where we talked about the Spirit speaking to us. As a result, the concept of hearing God's voice puzzled me. In recent years, however, I've started understanding it more. The Spirit has always been speaking to me, I've realized; I was just letting other things crowd him out. I was pushing the Spirit away.

I understand the Spirit as my helper, following John 14:26. "But the *Helper*, the Holy Spirit, whom the Father will send in my name, he will teach you all things and bring to your remembrance all that I have said to you" (NIV, italics and capitalization mine).

I love that Jesus commended the Spirit to us as our helper. I have learned that I really need a helper, especially when it comes to honing this skill of listening. He is the perfect helper because he is wiser than anyone on this earth, because he has a plan, and because he can shut down all the other voices that crowd my head and try to push his out.

Recent years brought me to the brink of exhaustion. Multiple cancer diagnoses made me question "Why?" Thankfully, that questioning and the exhaustion that came with it were temporary because I learned to slow down and listen to my "helper"— the one leading me toward wisdom and peace.

I learned to hear his comforting voice while I sat in hospitals receiving treatment after treatment. He strengthened me by reminding me not to put my hope in fleeting things of this world. And he comforted me so that I could comfort others —by being a presence of peace, and by listening to them like he listened to me.

I learned to start each day sitting in silence, often just staring out the window watching the sunrise, thanking him for the beauty of his creation and his good work in me.

I learned to take off the headphones or earbuds that prevented me from listening to the songbirds and the cars containing people who needed prayer.

I learned to stop and listen to those whom God had placed in my life when I didn't know how to handle yet another complicated story dividing my newsroom, my city, or the entire nation.

I learned to pause and consider the likely impact on my employees and our viewers of a decision I was mulling. Before delivering heartbreaking news to staff members about a beloved coworker's terminal diagnosis, I learned that the right words would come if I trusted the Spirit. The Spirit centered me and enabled me to convey the message to them with a still heart.

Here's what else I know: My helper shows up in nature. He shows up in people. He shows up in books and in my thoughts and dreams. When I choose to stop and listen to him, I realize that the Spirit is everywhere—in his word and in the people he has placed in my life.

I tried for so long to do it all by myself that I had forgotten I was supposed to yield to the Spirit. Now, when I yield to him, I'm in a position to receive the truth. That's when I get things right. I don't have a supernatural experience, nor do I typically hear a booming voice—though I can think of one life-saving instance in which I believe the voice of God literally saved me. That was the day I heard a voice in my head telling me not to go into a bathroom by myself days after one of my chemo treatments.

Here's what happened. I was going through my second round of chemotherapy, so I thought I knew what to expect this time around. I was exhausted and feeling crummy, but I thought it would be good to get out of the house for a while, so Michael and I went to a restaurant.

I had some soup and bread and felt incredibly thirsty. I then got a sharp headache followed by an intense desire to lie down. I thought I was going to vomit, so I told Michael I was going to go to the restroom. Halfway there, I heard a voice that said, "Don't go in there. Turn around." I did. I went back to the table and told Michael we needed to go outside.

Seconds later, Michael caught me as I passed out cold. My blood pressure had bottomed out, and I ended up spending a week in the hospital. Had I not listened to the Holy Spirit, I may have cracked my skull on the ceramic bathroom tile or been discovered too late to survive.

It wasn't a loud voice, but I know for sure it was the Spirit. I can't tell you how he will speak to you, just that he will. I know my helper is guiding me every day. I now also understand that I only learn from him when I stop to listen to him. When I do these things, that's when I make a difference. And that's also when I know I am doing the will of my Father.

Lessons Learned about Hearing Others

In their book, *The ONE Thing*, Gary Keller and Jay Papasan talk about choosing one thing to be your goal. They say everything you do should feed that "one thing" instead of allowing your purpose to be scattered or diluted. The authors write, "Extraordinary results are determined by how narrow you make your focus."[38]

That idea prompted me to take a different direction with planning. What was the "one thing" on which I could focus to make me a better wife, mother, boss, and follower of Jesus? Yep, listening. The sticky note that says "listen" remains on a work monitor as a daily reminder to do just that.

Michael and I have tried to teach the value of listening to our son by asking him how he is doing. When I first moved to Pittsburgh for my job, Price and Michael stayed behind in Oklahoma until the school semester ended. During our nightly calls, Price typically dove right in talking about himself and asking if I had found any new Pokémon characters. One day I said, "My day was great; how was yours?" He got the point. Or, I should say, his dad got the point, and the two had a conversation when the phone call was over. Soon enough, I started noticing my then six-year-old starting our daily conversations with, "Mom, how was your day?" Then he'd stop and wait for me to share while he listened patiently.

This week I'm on vacation. While I'm writing, he is playing on his Xbox with his friends. Every day I have heard him ask one of them, "How is your day so far?" Nearly every evening he'll ask me or his dad, "How was your day?" It's a simple four-word question that makes all the difference in the world to the people around him. The fact that he asks the question is not what makes me most proud; it's

---

[38] Gary Keller and Jay Papsan, *The ONE Thing: The Surprisingly Simple Truth Behind Extraordinary Results* (Austin: Bend Press, 2012), 10.

that he pauses and waits for an answer. Asking the question makes him a good communicator; waiting for a response makes him an exceptional human being.

Are you asking the questions and pausing for a response? I bet if you stopped and asked women their thoughts, and if you really listened to their answers, you'd find that some problems you've been working to solve may no longer be big problems. I also bet that if you asked girls or women what they believe they can do to serve the Lord versus what boys or men can do, their answers would tell you what they are absorbing about the value of their gifts in your workplace, home, and church.

Just as God planted you where you are right now, God planted the people who are in your life. Stop and listen to them.

Now stop and listen to your helper, the Spirit. What is he saying to you?

Take a deep breath or imagine you're sipping a good wine. If you're focused on listening to the right voice, the other voices won't matter as much.

ACTION ITEMS

1.   Ensure that you have curriculum for pre-teen and teenage boys and girls that includes topics like grace, love, and listening to the Spirit. Becoming familiar with them will help young people to get ahead of the issues they confront and that can linger into adulthood. Remember that at the root of people's inability to listen is often not fully comprehending God's love and grace for them as individuals.

2.   Offer personality assessments to help members of leadership teams understand and listen to each other.

3.   Speak up when someone makes a statement that is driven by biases for or against a gender.

4.   Take a nature walk or specific times to "listen"—by yourself or with others.

Self-Reflection Questions for Church Leaders

1. How good a listener do you perceive yourself to be? On what do you base this perception?

2. What systems or tools do you have in place to help you remember to listen? A sticky note? A daily devotion? Listening sessions in your congregation? Listening is often first an intentional act before it becomes a habit. What can you put in place to ensure you are listening to God and to the people in your church?

3. When did you last set aside time to listen?

4. To which aspiring female leader in your congregation can you turn when you next need advice?

5. Think of an incident in which you undermined a woman's credibility by your speech or actions. What will you do differently next time? How can you mend this relationship and help rebuild her confidence?

Self-Reflection Questions for Female Leaders

1. How good a listener do you perceive yourself to be? On what do you base this perception?

2. What systems or tools do you have in place to help you remember to listen? A sticky note? A daily devotion? A dinnertime tradition? When is the last time you asked someone for feedback? Listening is a habit you can develop. How can you ensure you are listening to the Spirit and to other people?

3. When did you last set aside time to listen?

4. In what ways do you notice your helper, the Holy Spirit, every day?

5. Into what habits have you fallen that multiply rather than reduce the voices that crowd out your helper's voice? How might wean yourself off those other voices?

9

Just Behave

Assault and discrimination are still part of many workplace cultures, but I'm grateful for the women who were brave enough to speak up and initiate change, initiate change, including through the "Me Too" movement. Acts of discrimination and abuse that were once accepted are no longer tolerated. The courts now punish predators and abusers. And corporate America has changed the dialogue happening in the workplace—thanks to the bravery of men and women who were victims.

Lessons Learned about the Rules

I am fortunate. I have had a successful career, and no man has ever made a sexual advance on me at work or demanded sexual favors of me in return for a promotion. Yet in 2016, well before the "Me Too" movement, a stunning 60 percent of women in United States workplaces reported they had experienced "unwanted sexual attention, sexual coercion, sexually crude conduct, or sexist comments in the workplace."[39] A 2021 study found that 81 percent of women and 43 percent of men reported experiencing some form of sexual harassment

---

[39] Chai R. Feldblum and Victoria A. Lipnic, "Select Task Force on the Study of Harassment in the Workplace," *U.S. Equal Employment Opportunity Commission,* June 2016, https://www.eeoc.gov/select-task-force-study-harassment-workplace#_ftn16.

and/or assault in their lifetime,[40] be that verbal harassment, cyber harassment, or sexual assault. Why?

A significant contributor is surely that men are still overwhelmingly the ones with the most power and authority in the workplace and in society more broadly and that they have made the rules by which all of us are meant to abide. When I say "overwhelmingly," here's what I mean: In 2021 the number of Fortune 500 companies with a female CEO hit a record high. The number was forty-one! Forty-one in total! In 2021 only slightly more than 8 percent of the leading companies had a female CEO.[41] That means that all the way up the career ladder there have been more men in leadership. Such a lack of diversity leads to blind spots and unconscious biases.

If you research the subject of bias, you will see many articles pointing to a 1989 study that focused on women working in a factory. This decades-old study compared women who were machinists to women on the assembly line. The reason those two groups were compared is that women were not traditionally machinists but worked the assembly line. At the time of the study, both groups of women dealt with the same number of men at work.

When *The New York Times* interviewed the study's author, Dr. Nancy Baker, a psychologist from Los Angeles, she said: "On all 28 items of a sexual harassment scale, ranging from lewd remarks to sexual assault, the women machinists had the highest scores. ... The more non-traditional the job for women, the more sexual harassment. Women surgeons and investment bankers rank among the highest for harassment."[42] In the same article Dr. Louise Fitzgerald, a psychologist

[40] Maria Clark, "70+ Sexual Harassment in the Workplace Statistics," *Etacktics,* November 4, 2021, https://etactics.com/blog/sexual-harassment-in-the-workplace-statistics.

[41] Courtney Connley, "A Record 41 Women are Fortune 500 CEOs—and for the First Time Two Black Women Made the List," *CNBC,* June 2, 2021, https://www.cnbc.com/2021/06/02/fortune-500-now-has-a-record-41-women-running-companies.html#:~:text=A%20record%2041.

[42] Daniel Goleman, "Sexual Harassment: It's About Power, Not Lust," *The New York Times,* October 22, 1991, www.nytimes.com/1991/10/22/science/sexual-harassment-it-s-about-power-not-lost.html.

at the University of Illinois, said this about women in the blue-collar workplace: "Men see women as invading a masculine environment. These are guys whose sexual harassment has nothing whatever to do with sex. They're trying to scare women off a male preserve."[43] Fitzgerald and others have said that in some cases men who grew up in male-dominated environments don't know how to act. I'd argue that that time has long passed and the excuses for poor behavior need to end.

I think we need to keep this in mind in our churches as we elevate and pursue women for leadership positions. Many are entering organizations and hierarchical structures that have long been dominated by men and probably still are. Christian men should know better. Understanding your power, living in humility, and loving women as sisters instead of objectifying them by viewing them as subjects of lust should keep men straight. But, dear brothers in Christ, in case you have any question about whether your jokes and comments about women are appropriate, let me remind you that if you have to question them, they're probably not. And in case you have any questions about whether it's okay to proposition a woman for sex and hold it over her for any reason, the answer is no. And if you are insecure about what letting a woman into the office means for how the vibe will change, the answer is get over it. Simply behave the way Jesus calls you to you behave. This means the days in which men made all the rules are over—and it may also mean the rules need to change. If you are a Christian, it may mean some reflection and repentance are in order.

Let's go a step further, though. It's time to eliminate any and all excuses. If we're going to move to a place where women have equal opportunities, we must get past the excuse that people can't control themselves, especially men. "Boys will be boys" is not an excuse for poor behavior. This is an issue of accountability and of what's in the heart. If the mandate is to love your neighbor—including women— as yourself and to regard them as sisters in Christ, then one could presume every man has the ability to get past the sexualization of women.

---

[43] Goleman, "Sexual Harassment."

Unfortunately, sexualization of women, which can be attributed to a lack of morality or spiritual compass, is not limited to the world outside the church. The church has been just as much a part of this shameful practice. In the church we talk about avoiding sexual immorality—as we should. But more fundamentally it's what dwells in our hearts that manifests in our choices and behaviors (Mark 7:20–23). So is it really love for others that motivates you? Is it treating others as Jesus did that motivates you? If not, then what is? It is our heart—our desires and motivations—that influences us to oppose God's intent, not the men and women conducting business together.

If we are obsessed with removing obstacles to keep people from sinning, then we're not addressing what's leading to the problem of sexual sin. Addressing this problem requires self-examination, repentance, and cleansing our hearts and minds. Why punish women with exclusion instead of expecting men to do those three things? The church bears some responsibility for the sexualization of women by allowing men to make excuses for their bad behavior and putting the blame for that behavior on the women. Excuses such as "She shouldn't have dressed that way" and "She shouldn't have been alone" are wholly inappropriate reasons for our failure to love one another as brothers and sisters. They merely make it easier for us to sin and to victimize others.

Lessons Learned about the Dangers of Exclusion

Rules and regulations based solely on gender typically prevent women from being assigned positions in which they can lead. As a young woman growing up in the church and as an adult volunteering today, I've experienced these limitations firsthand. Most of the churches I have attended have limited opportunities for women to lead because they don't agree theologically that women can have gifts of leadership or at most that such leadership gifts are limited to ministering to children and youth—the least powerful. To me, that seems paranoid. In contrast, the marketplace has trusted my capacity, giftedness, and moral fitness to lead without being sexually inappropriate.

Limiting the exposure men and women have to one another is also referred to as the "Billy Graham rule"[44] of never meeting one-on-one with a person of the opposite sex. While I admire Graham as an icon of the faith and for having lived free of controversy, I wonder if perhaps it was his devotion to scripture, creating a culture of accountability, or prioritizing time with his family that kept him on the straight and narrow. After all, Jesus himself wasn't afraid to meet alone with a woman, as we see from his conversation with the woman at the well (John 4:1–42). But it was to her, of all the people in the town, that Jesus chose to reveal himself. We might say Jesus looked at her as a sister in the faith who deserved the chance to hear the good news, not as an object of lust. He is our example.

Of course, fear of exclusion also happens in the work world. I recall the president of a company voicing a concern to the owner at a meeting. His concern? That he and other male colleagues were becoming so fearful of being accused of sexual misconduct that the only reasonable solution seemed to be to go back to a time when men hung out having cigars together or playing golf. What did the owner say? "Just behave." My heart beat with pride. His response reaffirmed to me that it's not the situation that causes people to sin: it's their decision to do so.

We are all capable of behaving. "No temptation has overtaken you except what is common to mankind. And God is faithful; he will not let you be tempted beyond what you can bear. But when you are tempted, he will also provide a way out so that you can endure it" (1 Cor. 10:13, NIV). God made us capable of withstanding sin and saying no when needed.

I am so passionate about this this topic because keeping women out of the room has kept women from leading, and that's wrong. Nowhere does scripture say that the gifts of the Spirit are distributed based on one's gender. Since leadership is a gift of the Spirit, we can conclude that leadership is gift-based, not gender-based. Paul writes

---

[44] Seth Dowland, "The 'Modesto Manifesto,'" *Christian History Magazine* 111 (2014), https://christianhistoryinstitute.org/magazine/article/the-modesto-manifesto/.

that "all these [gifts] are the work of one and the sane Sprit, and he distributes them to each one, just as he determines" (1 Cor. 12:11, NIV). Nothing is said about that determination being based on one's gender.

How do we fix this issue? By admitting when our churches have "boys' clubs" and acknowledging that, because of them, the church has for centuries prioritized men for jobs and specifically for leadership positions—and also by acknowledging that not all men are consciously aware of and subscribe to such patriarchal priorities. Workplaces are leading the way on redressing this imbalance. The church needs to catch up.

Lessons Learned about Letting the Women Join

Men are going to hang out together and enjoy a round of golf or drinks. Women are going to hang out with one another and enjoy trips, book clubs, manicures, and baby and wedding showers. I realize that. But ultimately there needs to be a boundary to differentiate between social outings and business meetings. If business decisions or deals come up in these environments, stop talking until you can include everyone.

How then do we give women the same opportunities without jeopardizing our integrity? A leader I know never does one-on-one business dinners with a woman, only breakfast or lunch. Why? He's aware that not only the woman but other people would likely view such a dinner as inappropriate. He never has a one-on-one business dinner with a man, either.

One of my direct reports told me he was going to start meeting regularly with two of his team members—a woman and a man. The woman he'd be taking to lunch, the man to dinner. When asked why, he said he didn't want anyone thinking the meeting with the woman was in any way inappropriate. I affirmed his decision to protect himself, that female employee, and the station. But then I advised him that spending time with men but not women employees in what could be regarded as a social situation could create just as many problems. My advice: Be fair. Take both to lunch, and take them together, as this provides an extra layer of protection and accountability.

As leaders, it also behooves us to protect personal and family time. Why do workplace affairs happen? Largely out of convenience. We Christian leaders and employers can do our part to strengthen our employees' home lives. If our employees are overworked, obsessed with their jobs, and not at home, their home lives are inevitably going to suffer in one way or another. And if things are not good at home for one person on the team, I'd wager others are likely in the same boat. They have their work in common, often seem to understand each other better than their spouse does, and one thing leads to another. We can help prevent inappropriate relationships by encouraging our leaders and employees to take time away from work to have a healthy life.

To prevent awkward situations for women in our work environments, we should have more than one female leader. This will help us not only to have better organizations, but also to elevate *all* of God's children, men and women.

Now or later if you find yourself in a situation that could harm your personal or church family, if you are struggling in your relationships, if you feel tempted to overstep boundaries, talk to a trusted friend, church leader, or a counselor.

Dear church, the goal is to make *both* protection *and* inclusion happen. How can we make sure we put parameters in place that are cautious but reasonable? And how can we include men and women in the same leadership circles without excluding some for fear they can't control themselves?

By having honest conversations. By examining our hearts. By welcoming more than one woman inside our leadership circles.

ACTION ITEMS

1. Evaluate your church's policies on where men and women are allowed to meet. What should remain? What should be altered?

2. Create policies that prevent business decisions from being made during social gatherings that do not include all relevant persons.

3. Evaluate how much you expect people to be away from their families or friends and how much work is impinging on that family or friend time. Yes, it is part of the job, but ensure you are not abusing someone's availability and causing unnecessary strain on their personal life.

4. Instead of assuming men and women are tempted by each other, provide resources that remind folks of their primary identity and relationship as brothers and sisters in the faith.

Self-Reflection Questions for Church Leaders

1. Does your church have a "good ol' boys" culture in church leadership? If so, what steps can you take to dismantle it and be more inclusive of women with leadership gifting?

2. Where or when might women of your church have felt uncomfortable as the only female in the room? What could you do differently next time?

3. How have we hurt or hindered our leaders by creating unnecessary strain on their families?

4. Is there an implication in our teaching/by-laws that men can't control themselves around women? If so, what ought we to change in order to mitigate the lie that these messages and practices perpetuate?

Self-Reflection Questions for Female Leaders

1. What steps have you taken to include more women in your organization and dismantle any "good ol' boys" culture?

2. What are you doing to include other women in decision-making?

3. How can you help forge bonds among female leaders without creating a "girls' club"?

SECTION 3

Employing Personal Care and Growth Strategies

10

Do Your Best

Before I turned forty, my dear colleague Bilte told me this next part of my life was going to be amazing simply because I would finally stop caring so much about what others think. Now that I'm closer to fifty, I can tell you he was right. In fact, I smile when I see the social media posts of my friends in their thirties who feel like they have it all figured out. Those posts remind me that while I had learned so much, when I was that age, there was so much I had yet to experience. Their posts make me think, "You don't know what you don't know." Likewise, when I hear advice from people who are older than me, like my parents, my mother-in-law, and my grandparents, who say, "If only *I* could be forty-five again. *You* still have half your life ahead of you," I realize it's true: I do!

I certainly do care a lot less about things that used to consume me in my younger years. I still watch my weight, but it's more for health reasons than trying to be a size four again. And while I like to buy clothes to look sharp, now I do so to project an executive presence. If I'm at home, I'm quite happy in jeggings and T-shirts. As an extremely fair-skinned woman, I admit I'm still on a quest to find the perfect self-tanner, but that's mostly because I find it hard to accept my ivory pale skin when it comes to donning shorts in the summer months.

I have finally started to embrace my naturally curly hair. (To be honest, it took losing my hair twice to chemo to embrace those curls.) I'm directionally challenged, but whereas in my younger years I typically hid that from my travel companions, now I tell them upfront so they don't ask me to navigate.

I spent decades fighting the fact that I am an emotional person—until I finally accepted myself as I am. Don't talk to me about my emotions. It makes me highly emotional. It just does.

I still struggle with sins of the tongue. In *The Me I Want to Be: Becoming God's Best Version of You,* John Ortberg talks about "signature" sins, a term he attributes to author Michael Mangis. A signature sin is a sin one can attribute to one's unique life patterns, temperaments, and gifts. Ortberg usefully observes that the areas of our gifts and passions most often indicate our areas of highest vulnerability. He writes, "Extroverts who can encourage and inspire others can also be attracted to gossip."[45] That's me. I'm a team builder. I love to speak to crowds. I love to inspire. But if I'm not careful, those same passions and gifts can also lead me down the path of gossip and vanity.

I'm a people pleaser, and over the years I've realized that's at the root of many of my sins. I've always been able to spot that tendency in other people and to call it out quickly. Thanks to good bosses, I've learned I have the very same faults. I remember calling out someone for overworking and not taking care of themselves, and my boss, Ray, saying, "Suz, but you just did the very same thing."

I've learned that although most of the ways I try to please others are "good," when I do them to earn approval from a boss or from God, they're not a reflection of God's grace. Until I accepted that God finds me worthy of his love, that in fact I cannot earn it, I likewise expected colleagues to prove their worth through their deeds rather than loving them as they are.

You have God's approval simply because he made you and loves you. You should do good works because you love him and you want to display his goodness and mercy to others. You can't earn your way to heaven by doing good: Jesus did it for you.

---

[45] John Ortberg, *The Me I Want to Be* (Grand Rapids, MI: Zondervan, 2010), 147.

This chapter is not going to tell of how my people-pleasing stopped in the newsroom. Because it didn't. But it was in a newsroom that I learned how much of a hold this sin had on me. It was in a newsroom that I grasped that God is the only one I must please. And it was in a newsroom that I hit bottom emotionally.

In my quest to earn everyone's approval, my worrying and nights of crying had taken me to a low point. It was a process that had repeated itself for decades. I'd find a niche or move to a new job. I'd do well; I got results (meaning good station ratings). But in the process I'd get exhausted. When things were going great, I was great. When things were not going great, neither was I. And while people at work knew I was grumpy, the people at home were the ones bearing the brunt of my exhaustion.

It happened spectacularly when I moved to Fort Myers, Florida, in my early twenties. I was uncertain about whether I fit in newscasting. I had also just gone through a breakup and was a mess. Thanks to a good employee assistance program, I sought counseling. I sat in that counselor's office and told her what the young man had told me when he broke up with me: "I've been putting you on a pedestal, and nothing is making you happy. I'm emotionally exhausted."

I agree that he had put me on a pedestal. He spent his free time with me. He helped me in any way he could with work projects and home projects. He made it a priority to help me get what I wanted for my career and life. And, indeed, little of that was making me happy. In my defense, "nothing" was too strong a word to describe my lack of fulfillment in the relationship or with him. But I couldn't argue with how *he* felt. And he apparently felt exhausted by trying to be what I needed. Then my counselor dropped a bomb. "How would you respond to the statement: 'You are currently emotionally exhausting to the people closest to you'?"

I couldn't deny it. I was exhausting to my boyfriend, who just wanted to be with me. I was exhausting to my mom, who took my emotional calls twenty-four hours a day. I was exhausting to my friends, who had to endure the overflow of my emotions. I was exhausting even to myself.

You could say I just needed help; but, folks, let me tell you: I was creating drama because I was trying to earn everyone's approval. I was even trying to win the approval of the boyfriend who claimed I exhausted him emotionally. I was trying to be pretty enough to him, and in some ways I think I believed the career help he was offering me was a way for me to prove myself to him as well. My perfectionism came through kicking and screaming even when it was disguised as burdensome.

My perfectionism had created anxiety and depression in my life. To help get myself out of my deepest valley, I turned to medication and years of counseling. The drama subsided for a time but continued to play out from my twenties well into my forties, when I finally understood that this need to earn others' approval extended even to my faith life. Whenever things weren't right, I believed it was a result of me not doing enough. For a very long time, I never felt as if I was sufficient.

You may not identify with my level of people-pleasing addiction, but I imagine the majority of people struggle with it at some level. Just listen to what women describe as draining their energy when you talk in groups. Hear their complaints and motives. Look at Pinterest—and, frankly, all social media platforms. Each of these venues screams of a woman's plight to get approval from others. Unfortunately, Christians in particular seem to struggle with this.

Lessons Learned about People-Pleasing Women

Why is it that so many Christian women are people pleasers? Consider the roles women typically fill in the home and in the marketplace, and identify which are situational or simply unhealthy cultural norms. God made many women to be nurturing, and such women fill those typical gender roles and responsibilities easily. If you believe God's instruction to women to serve their husbands is clear, then I have a follow-up question for you: What does serving your husband look like for you? Scripture doesn't seem to define this in absolutes.

For example, I'd argue that in our household I serve my son and husband by having a good job and providing for them. Sometimes this necessitates working long days, and sometimes it provides perks and benefits that also show care and service to my family. I don't believe that just because I'm a woman it is my ordained role to come home after work and do all of the cooking and cleaning. There is no established list of "to do" items based on gender. Long ago Michael and I came to an agreement regarding each of our responsibilities, and we renegotiate these things from time to time. We have created rhythms, tasks, and boundaries to honor each other's giftedness and to prioritize our service to one another.

I'll go into the topic of boundaries more deeply in chapter 11. But I believe we do need to grapple with it a bit right here.

At the root of the struggle of trying to be pleasing is often a boundary problem. My therapist assigned me the task of reading Henry Cloud and John Townsend's book *Boundaries*. In it, they address the common myth that boundaries are sign of disobedience:

> God is more concerned with our hearts than he is with our outward compliance. "For I desire mercy, not sacrifice, and acknowledgment of God rather than burnt offerings" (Hos 6:6) In other words, if we say yes to God or anyone else when we really mean no, we move into a position of compliance, and that is the same as lying.[46]

Because God is more concerned with our hearts, we each need to answer: What's in your heart? And: Where is the Spirit leading you? Your responses will show whether you are agreeing to things because you believe they're part of God's will or because you are worried about what someone else will think. If I agree to take on an extra project because I care more about what my peers and direct reports will think than about how good it might be for my team's growth to handle the project without me, then I'm essentially elevating my self-importance and enabling my need for others' approval. And if I go into work on a day off instead of listening to the Spirit when he tells me I need rest, I am overstepping the boundary lines God has given to me for my own

---

[46] Henry Cloud and John Townsend, *Boundaries* (Grand Rapids, MI: Zondervan, 1992), 110.

welfare and prioritizing my need for others to see how hardworking I am. Both of these scenarios are evidence of my approval-seeking heart's inclination to disobey. I disobey when I idolize success and others' opinions of me.

Underlying a lack of boundaries is the belief that I'm never enough. It's a belief that I need to earn love, as a result of which I put myself in situations in which I overstep my own boundaries in order to feel worthy.

How do you know whether you're acting out of the wrong motives? It's tricky, and achieving clarity takes practice. For example, if I say yes to something like a project at church or work, that doesn't necessarily mean I'm blurring boundaries or trying to earn your love. I am an Enneagram three, and my love language is gift-giving. I'm actually wired to give my best all the time—to everyone, in every situation. I'm an achiever and a maximizer. But I also know these gifts can lead to overwork, selfishness, and relentless pleasing.

Can you pinpoint a particular insecurity that pushes you to overcompensate by people-pleasing? Failing to have boundaries, coupled with an inclination to seek to please others, can actually prevent others from reaching their God-given potential. If we're doing things for others and pulling all of the extra duty, we're not allowing someone else to shine. I know it's not loving if I convey to others that they can't do something on their own. In fact, it's plain selfish.

Lessons Learned about Finding Peace

The opposite of living on a rollercoaster of approval-seeking is being grounded in peace. I first became aware of such peace when I was going through one of my toughest personal times. Michael and I had lived in Tampa for less than two years, and I'd just left a job. I was at a low point in my life. I was searching for fulfillment, knowing that relationally and spiritually I was impoverished. It was a tough time for our careers and for our marriage. The career stuff was tough because things at home weren't happy. Michael and I had finally realized we had entered into our marriage as two people who were not on the same page about faith, family, and the future. Still, I'm grateful that during that time the Spirit prompted me to surround myself with good, believing people at church and at work. Those believers at work in particular kept me on a more even keel.

It wasn't through one of those believers that I realized people notice how you respond to tough times. Instead, it was through a random producer. She came up to me on a particularly difficult day and said, "I don't know what is going on in your personal life, and I really don't care to hear about it. But it is obvious there is something about you that gives you peace." I regret not circling back and befriending that producer, but I'm incredibly grateful she reminded me that even in our toughest times, we believers have a presence of peace—the Holy Spirit—who can stabilize and ground us no matter what's going on around us.

Friends, peace comes from being reminded there is more to life than your present circumstances and there is one who is looking out for you. Recall what Philippians 4:6–7 says: "Do not be anxious about anything, but in every situation, by prayer and petition, with thanksgiving, present your requests to God. And the peace of God, which transcends all understanding, will guard your hearts and your minds in Christ Jesus" (NIV). Rather than expend your energy on pleasing people, take your concerns and your lack to God in prayer. The ensuing peace is one that only God can give and one that will guard your heart.

The past few years have been trying ones for me. I have experienced changes in my company, a second cancer diagnosis, and the COVID-19 pandemic and have tried to report sensitively and justly the racial injustice and riots in my city and a national election in which my city and state became a focal point. And those are just the headlines.

It was also a rough year for me as a leader of my staff. The aforementioned events weren't merely news stories that my staff covered as part of their jobs; they were stories that hit home. My colleagues personally experienced their race and profession being attacked—all while risking their health to continue covering the news.

For a while there was hardly a week in which I was not delivering grim news to my staff about a colleague or one of their loved ones falling ill.

How did I cope? I regularly poured out my heart to one of my friends, who is also the leader of my discipleship group. On one such occasion, Janie said, "I'm so glad you can be a 'presence of peace' for your staff." Her statement struck me because it awakened me to the fact that that's precisely what I had been doing. By contrast, when we were going through big changes in our company, another leader had described me as being a "Pollyanna." That leader interpreted my calm and even cheerful response as a sign that I hadn't understood the gravity of the situation and was being naïve about what was about to unfold. I wasn't being a Pollyanna; I knew exactly what was going on. But I deliberately opted not to flounder in sorrow or frustration. Those words in Philippians about a peace that surpasses understanding encouraged me to refuse to be anxious and instead to give the situation to God. Those words reminded me that God has a plan even when things are hard. By internalizing those words, I actually feel a peace that non-believers don't understand. I refuse to succumb to the apparent awfulness of the situation by reminding myself that God is in control. He hears my worries, and je will guide me through the tough times. That knowledge guards my heart from any future anxieties as well.

Dear friends, you cannot trust this peace from God if your motive is to please the folks who don't have that same peace. Their anxiety will drive you to sin, whether by disobeying God's will for you, saying hurtful words, or not taking care of your God-given body.

In the hard years to which I referred above, one phrase kept me going: "Be a presence of peace." I repeated it over and over in my head on particularly challenging days. Being a presence of peace requires work. It requires prayer. It requires listening to God. It requires reading the Word. It requires spending time with people who are wiser than you. It requires Sabbath rest. And it requires grace for onself and others.

Lessons Learned about Grace

For me, and maybe for you, having a presence of peace comes down to accepting God's grace. Paul describes in 2 Corinthians 12:9

that Jesus said to him: "My grace is sufficient for you, for my power is made perfect in weakness." "Therefore, [says Paul,] I will boast all the more gladly about my weaknesses, so that Christ's power may rest on me." Paul's words remind me that I don't have to be perfect. In fact, they're a good reminder that I never will be.

I remember sitting in a newsroom one day frustrated that we were once again in a tense ratings battle with our competition. The pressure from everyone up the chain was immense. A colleague could see the pressure all over my face. Her advice to me? "You'll be better off when you realize that no matter by how much we win the ratings war, we will never be good enough."

She may have been right. But to God I am always enough. When people ask how I can maintain the pace I do, or when they wonder how I can face one medical challenge after another, I tell them it's because I know I am loved. Because I know I'm loved, I can embrace my weakness—for the weaker I am, the more I rely on God's strength. That is the unique opportunity God has given me in newsrooms. My colleagues have seen me tackle situations that would have made some people crumble, but by and large I don't, and I can be a presence of peace.

If you are relying on your own strength or the personal strength of others, you will be disappointed. It is only through Christ that you are strong.

During my medical crises, I learned suffering does not mean I have done something wrong in God's eyes. We see numerous examples in scripture of God declaring that suffering, sadness, and illness are not always consequences of sin. In fact, when questioned about the source of a child's physical illness, Jesus insisted it was neither the result of his sin nor that of his parents (John 9:3). Likewise, my cancer bouts were not God punishing me. God's plan for me may not be all sunshine and roses, and it may not always take the form for which I hope. But God's plan has purpose, for "we know that in all things God works for the good of those who love him, who have been called according to his purpose" (Rom. 8: 28, NIV). Notice that Paul says God has a plan in *all* things. Not in some things or only in the happy things. God works in the bad things, too. And this work is always for the "good of those who love him." By this Paul means whatever is God's ultimate good for you—which is to glorify him for all eternity. The "good" is not necessarily something that produces happiness in the moment, offers a pain-free life, or promises financial success. The "good" is God's grace at work in and through you for our benefit.

This isn't the first time I've talked about grace in this book, and it won't be the last, because mid-forties Suzanne loves talking about God's grace. It was because I did not understand this gift of God's grace that for years I was a highly emotional person running around trying to gain everyone's approval, including God's. I had to reach a point of exhaustion—not once, but three times—before I finally understood God's grace.

Ultimately, God always gives us more than a "Well done!" from our bosses or peers. He gives us more than money or things. He gives us undeserved love expressed through unmerited grace.

Lessons about the Church Fueling People-Pleasing

Dear church, let's face it: We have been guilty of fueling the engines of people-pleasers in order to get things done. I'm not saying this has come from a bad place. On the contrary, I think we don't even realize we are doing it because we rely on volunteers and people to step up and take their places in the body of believers. In Ephesians 4:12, Paul tells us it's our job to prepare God's people for works of service. But if we aren't careful, our push for service and filling certain volunteer roles also come from a belief that we must teach our girls they are "good" if they serve—which they do by making others happy.

How are we doing at raising the children in our congregations? Proverbs 22:6 reminds us to raise our children in a way so they carry the lessons we teach them into adulthood. (ESV). Are we training our children to examine their hearts and embrace God's love? Are we training them to look and see how Jesus lived so they can be his hands and feet each day? Are we training them to do good things because they *are* Christians, not in order to *be* Christians? Are we training our boys to do the same good things and serve others? Or are we training them to believe they should always be served?

This balance of serving out of obedience and not people-pleasing is a tricky thing to navigate if we're not starting with the heart and fostering genuine, healthy relationships in our churches.

I finally found this balance when I formed some healthy relationships with other women who understood the inner turmoil of needing approval. These were women who knew how to sacrifice and who loved to serve others from a place of genuine love for God rather than in an effort to assuage their own insecurities or inadequacies or to earn approval.

As I formed good, genuine relationships with these frank women, I started trusting them and I started trusting God more. I learned to trust that he does love me. And I started trusting that he has a plan for me that is more expansive than the exhausting tight spiral of working to gain others' approval.

God loves me, and he loves you. The joy of the Lord is my strength, and it's yours too. Joy from the wins of pleasing others is short term. Long-term joy is from our good God. Friends, your time on earth is short. There is only one "well done" you should be aiming to receive: God's. He longs for you to love him, to spend time with him, to know that he has your back, and to accept his love. His love and approval are so much better than what the world asks of you in exchange for an incomplete and imperfect love. For God's love and approval are grace—a gift. You cannot earn such a gift, just as you cannot earn everyone's approval. Do your best. Follow God's voice. Make time for him. You are enough for him.

ACTION ITEMS

1. Talk to our kids about grace from a young age.
2. Make Christian counseling readily available to people. Explain that feelings of needing to prove oneself or not accepting all of God's love are feelings they can (and

should) work out with a counselor before they lead to other problems.

3. To identify areas of strengths and to help spot areas of vulnerability, offer Enneagram, StrengthsFinder, or other personality assessments, especially for leaders.

Self-Reflection Questions for Church Leaders

1. How have you fostered people-pleasing in your congregation?

2. In what ways have you taught that we serve *because* we are Christians or that we serve *to be* Christians (particularly among your children)?

3. In what ways is your church a "presence of peace" in your community?

Self-Reflection Questions for Female Leaders

1. With whom can you work to examine your motives at work, at home, and at church?

2. What inhibits you from being honest about your struggle with people-pleasing?

3. How does how you are wired lead you to please people in ways that make you vulnerable to sinning?

4. What steps can you take to ensure you are a presence of peace for others?

11

Live in the Margins

If ever there was a year that magnified my struggle with maintaining boundaries, it was 2020. In looking back at the advent of the COVID-19 pandemic, I bet a lot of you feel that way too. It's extremely challenging not to blur boundary lines when for months on end work life, school life, home life, and even church life all take place within the same walls. Though I wish I could say being restricted to the same small space as my family during that time was a gift, they weren't always quality hours we spent together.

Price is not like his mom when it comes to using a lot of words. That was very true during the quarantine when I asked him how his day was, his answer was usually, "Good." Then I'd ask, "What did you do that was good?" He would answer, "School stuff." And despite my own weariness, I'd try to get more by prodding. But I quickly realized I wasn't going to find out much in those conversations. It was when Price prayed at night that I really learned what he was observing and experiencing. He often prayed, "Dear God, help Mom not to be so stressed." Thankfully now that prayer is mostly reserved for his hybrid teacher.

I know Price heard and witnessed my work stress at home a lot more than usual during the pandemic. For his entire life he's been the child of parents who work in news, so he has always overheard heavy conversations with staff, agents, and bosses. We have had to answer calls at all times of the day, and he's seen us leave ordinary family moments to run to the TV to see difficult events unfolding. The surface stuff of chaos in our work wasn't new. What was new was that, because I was working from home, often from 8:00 a.m. until 7:30 p.m., he overheard the newsroom banter all day long on our Teams chat. And because the content of that news banter was consistently more serious than he had ever heard before—with not only scary pandemic announcements and weather emergencies, but mass shootings, racial insurrections, and even an attack on the nation's Capitol on January 6, 2021—it was not a great time for or with my boy. He was constantly shutting the door to my office because what was going on inside was too loud and disturbing for him to concentrate. Nor was I spending more time with him, for with the exception of more family dinners together, I got fewer breaks at home than I did by physically going into the newsroom. The boundaries between work and home had dissolved almost completely. We never seemed to have any time off. And that was all incredibly stressful for our family.

Memories of my upbringing as a preacher's kid seeped back. My experience was that there rarely seemed to be any time off. But I do remember two things that enabled my dad to "disconnect": sports, specifically Cubs games during the day before Wrigley Field allowed lights in the stadium, and our big vacations. We had a pop-up camper and put stickers of each state we visited on the back. We'd take two weeks each year and travel—to Niagara Falls, Mount Rushmore, the Smoky Mountains, and other wonderful places. The fact that those trips happened before cell phones and social media made it much easier for my mom and dad to disconnect than it is for us nowadays. I remember that my dad would get up early every morning to make us breakfast and that after that he'd bring out his briefcase with whatever he was reading. My brother and I said once, "See, Dad's always working." That's when our mom explained, "That's not work. That's your dad making time with God a priority."

You know something really made an impression when you remember it so vividly thirty years later. And that's the case for those vacations. They really meant something to my formation.

The pressures of leadership, whether in a church or in the marketplace, are difficult to escape. Always being there for the people I lead is a real struggle for me, especially in a society that doesn't encourage people to take a day off. But over time I've learned to set some boundaries, as my dad did.

Lessons Learned about What Boundaries Are

Setting boundaries means knowing when to say yes and when to say no—and sticking with it. I've become better at leaving work behind when I go home, turn off the phone, and trust others to make decisions.

Why is this topic worth an entire chapter? We cannot sustain the pace at which we are going without having healthy boundaries. Moreover, healthy boundaries are required of effective kingdom builders. If we are totally exhausted from being pulled in different directions or areas where God doesn't want us to focus, we cannot follow the path on which He has set each of us. Failing to follow healthy boundaries is caving to temptation.

Christian counseling introduced me to the term *boundaries*. My counselor referred me to Henry Cloud and John Townsend's book *Boundaries*, which I mentioned earlier. Many of us Christians have blurred the lines between service and obedience. Our calendars are packed to unhealthy levels, "church stuff" included. We're so afraid of saying no and offending someone that we say yes"to the point of burnout. Cloud and Townsend speak to us in our chaos:

Made in the image of God, we were created to take responsibility for certain tasks. Part of taking responsibility, or ownership, is knowing what is our job, and what isn't. Workers who continually take on duties that aren't theirs will eventually burn out. It takes wisdom to know what we should be doing and what we shouldn't.[47]

---

[47] Henry Cloud and John Townsend, *Boundaries: When to Say Yes, How to Say No to Take Control of Your Life* (Grand Rapids: Zondervan, 1992), 27.

It's true! Saying yes to the things to which God has called us and no to the people and things to which God has *not* called us keeps us on the right path to fulfilling our purposes.

For example, while we can contribute to others' walk with Jesus, we are not responsible for another person's walk. They are. I equate this to hiring people in a newsroom. I can talk to job candidates, I can have several managers talk to those job candidates, and I can vet them to the highest level. We can train them, and we can give them all the tools they need to succeed. At the end of the day, though, it's up to that person to decide if they are going to succeed. There's only so much I can do as a manager or leader. If an employee chooses not to use the tools given them and what they learned from their mentors, that is their choice.

My own boundary journey took me to Galatians 5:13: "You, my brothers and sisters, were called to be free. But do not use your freedom to indulge the flesh; rather, serve one another humbly in love" (NIV). Paul is saying that we are free, that we don't have to earn God's love, that he gives us grace sufficient to every day. A servant's heart is motivated by humility and love, not an incessant desire to please and gain approval, a desire that prevents them from saying no, drawing a line.

Over the years, I've gotten things jumbled in my people-pleasing, making-things-happen brain. I'm a believer in leaders serving and not putting themselves first. This does *not* mean enabling and doing for others things that they should be doing for themselves. How do we know if we are enabling? Let's look at the alternative—what it means to love others truly and to help them live out their God-given purpose.

Merriam-Webster has quite a few definitions of love. When you read the "full definition," number four is what we are talking about: an "unselfish loyal and benevolent concern for the good of another."[48] It prompts us to have "benevolent concern" for others. Merriam-Webster then defines benevolent as "organized for the purpose of doing good."[49]

---

[48] *Merriam-Webster Dictionary*, "love," accessed January 31, 2022, https://www.merriam-webster.com/dictionary/love.

[49] *Merriam-Webster Dictionary*, "benevolent," accessed January 31, 2022, https://www.merriam-webster.com/dictionary/benevolent.

We're talking about doing the best for the other person. We're talking about helping others reach their God-given potential.

I've had to set boundaries for myself in this area. I followed bad advice for many years. Once, after I'd missed a few days of work, a news director pointed out to me that "if nobody could tell if I was there or not, then I wasn't needed any day." As a young leader I took that to mean I needed to "do" things for my staff every day to make my presence felt. That led to a pattern of enabling and holding others back. By contrast, the best piece of advice I heard was from one of my biggest mentors, Marian, who said: "It took a long time to learn that the better my team did without me, the better job I was doing at leading them." She was right.

What it takes to do that is humility. It means thinking more about others and less about yourself. It takes really wanting the best long-term outcome for the other. Marian told me the fact that my team executed our playbook during a hurricane, while I was stuck on a cruise ship, showed I had led and taught them well. She knew I would think it reflected poorly on me if they hadn't done well while I was away. She also knew I would wonder if they had done better because I wasn't there. It takes humility to make success about your team rather than about you. It also takes trust. Trust and humility go hand in hand. And I still have to work on both.

For five and a half years I worked as a morning executive producer in Atlanta. It's still the longest time anyone has spent in that position because it is so exhausting. I was at the station by 11 p.m. every night and I didn't leave until at least 9 a.m. the next day. I was the only manager on duty, so the stress was high.

After my years on that shift the station added a 4 p.m. newscast, and I finally got to move off that night shift. I was ecstatic. I was moving up, and they were going to bring in someone else to take the reins for the night shift. The problem was that my overnight team struggled with the transition, and the show suffered. Even worse, our ratings suffered. About five months later I had to go back to the morning shift, where I stayed for six more months.

In the time away, however, I learned that I had been doing too much in the night shift position. I had built a great team atmosphere, but my overzealous contributions in areas in which my colleagues should have managed themselves actually had hurt the team. When I returned, I was very intentional about not getting in the "weeds" as much. I wrote fewer stories, and I let other people make decisions. In doing so, I finally made room for others to take ownership and grow. Isn't that what a leader is supposed to do? At least the kind of leader who cares for their team.

I write this as I'm on vacation—a vacation during which I'm not checking emails to see what decisions my colleagues made about newscast coverage. I'm not checking the station website. I have this privilege of truly being on vacation while I'm on vacation because I have worked hard to create personal boundaries for myself and my family and because I've created boundaries to let my leaders lead and grow. After all, that's why I hired them, and that's what I've coached them to do. Yet when I'm in the office, I still serve my team. I'm not above answering a phone. I'm not above ordering food myself or setting food out on the table for them. I'm not above helping when my help is needed. But every day I must ask myself: "Am I actually helping others by jumping in? Or am I hindering someone's opportunity to grow?" The newsroom has taught me to set boundaries.

Lessons Learned about Honoring Those Who Set Boundaries

Once you've taken inventory of the areas in which you have been lacking boundaries, the natural next step is to establish boundaries. Then you have to articulate them to the people they will affect. Once all that is established, you start living by them. Awesome, right? Well, it should be. But I've learned others can hold resentment of sorts against you if they don't like how your boundaries affect them or if they can't set boundaries for themselves. Perhaps the issue is figuring out hours to attend a child's games or doctors' appointments, or perhaps it's about taking a sabbath. In such situations, you must lead by example. Trust your people. Go to your kid's ballgame. Take your kid to their doctor's appointment. Take a sabbath. And make it possible for others to do the same.

This takes practice. I remember one boss nudging me: "Suz, you think that the newsroom folks are admiring the hours you work and the things you are giving up for your job? They aren't. They think you're crazy."

He was right. They did. I had to lead by example by setting and keeping boundaries. Then I had to help people create boundaries of their own. I had to honor those boundaries. And I had to praise them publicly for doing so. That's how you create a culture that honors healthy boundaries.

Lessons Learned about Honoring Boundaries at Church

I learned a lot about creating boundaries in newsrooms. I've seen some leaders do it well and others not so much. The same goes for what I've seen in churches. I've seen pastors who couldn't stop saying yes, and their families suffered. I've seen pastors who were awesome about teaching about and keeping the Sabbath and identifying people's specific gifts and making sure they were used in the way God intended.

Dear church, we need to be leaders in creating healthy boundaries. We particularly need to do so for our churches to embrace female leaders because women are already pulled in so many directions. While the church gets accustomed to having women in leadership positions, we can support women by helping them to maintain those clear boundaries. In an effort to seize any opportunity to lead, boundaries for women in the church may get further blurred—by the women themselves or by the rest of us—and the result is burnout for them, their families, and those around them.

Newsrooms and ministry have burnout in common. I've found we can avoid burnout if we all respect one another's time off. A survey conducted by Limeade in October 2020 found that 72 percent of workers say they're feeling burned out, compared to 42 percent of those surveyed in October 2019.[50] Managers are feeling stretched thin. Of those managers, 59 percent said they're working more than they did before the pandemic, and 72 percent said they're under pressure to work even when they're sick.[51] The problem is that remote working eliminated sick days. The boundaries have become blurred. People are afraid to say no, so they keep saying yes.

The church is no different. An article on the website for M1 Psychology cites a 2013 study from the Schaeffer Institute. It states that 1,700 pastors leave the ministry each month, citing depression, burnout, or being overworked as the primary reasons. According to the study, 90 percent of pastors report working fifty-five to seventy hours a week, and 50 percent of them feel unable to meet the demands of the job. The article goes on to cite these reasons for the burnout:

1. Being on call 24/7
2. Criticism and poor conflict resolution skills
3. Trying to please everyone or solve everyone's problems
4. Not delegating tasks
5. Poor social networks
6. Not being equipped for all aspects of ministry
7. Limited social life outside the church[52]

I am guessing those stats haven't changed much over the past decade, if at all. To keep good people in the church, we need to remember boundaries are an expression of love for ourselves and for others. When we are giving and serving out of love, we can be cheerful. "Each of you should give what you have decided in your heart to give,

---

[50] Danielle Andrus, "Pandemic Driving Up Employee Burnout Rates: Employees Feel Responsible," *Benefits Pro,* October 20, 2020, https://www.benefitspro.com/2020/10/20/pandemic-driving-up-employee-burnout-rates-managers-feel-responsible/?slreturn=20210729181635.

[51] Jack Craver, "Has the Internet Killed Sick Days?" *Benefits Pro,* January 18, 2019, https://www.benefitspro.com/2019/01/18/has-the-internet-killed-sick-days/.

[52] Julie Fickel, "Burnout in Pastors and Church Leadership," *M1Psychology,* accessed January 31, 2022, https://m1psychology.com/burnout-in-pastors-and-church-leadership/.

not reluctantly or under compulsion, for God loves a cheerful giver" (2 Corinthians 9:7, NIV).

Whether it happens in a newsroom or a church, doing things that others should be doing for themselves enables the blurring—or breaking—of boundaries. If we are running ourselves ragged, keeping others from reaching their God-given potential, or are not cheerful, we are not loving others as God intended.

Love yourself, and love those you lead by setting boundaries for yourself and honoring them.

ACTION ITEMS

1. If you are a church leader, set up some courses on setting and keeping boundaries, especially for your leadership team. If you are a female leader and no one is doing this for you, do it for yourself.

2. Identify what you are doing that someone else should be doing for themselves and for their growth.

3. Identify where you have lacked or broken your boundaries. Create a plan to establish or fix them. You may need to seek the help of a trusted leader for this.

4. Set up rewards for those in your organization who have set/kept boundaries.

5. Honor boundaries when someone on your team sets them.

6. Create an on-call system or other needed systems in your workplace so people can set boundaries while making sure business still gets done.

Self-Reflection Questions for Church Leaders

1. Where can you lead by example in setting boundaries?

2. Where have you crossed boundaries set by someone on your team?

3. What practices or systems do you have that may make it harder for women on your team to keep the same kind of boundaries that men keep?

4. When did you last discuss boundaries with your team?

Self-Reflection Questions for Female Leaders

1. What boundaries do you need to create in your work or home life?

2. How can you help people on your team establish and keep boundaries?

3. Are you honoring your team members' boundaries? In what ways can you do this better?

4. How can you communicate the successes of your team members that are the result of maintaining good boundaries?

12

Learn to Rest

I find it no coincidence that I'm writing a chapter on the Sabbath on my vacation—while I'm resting from my day job. The two big stuffed "Energizer Bunnies" in my office testify to how difficult I find it to rest. Marian, my boss and leader for many years, nicknamed me "the Energizer Bunny" when I was in my early thirties. She always said, "Suzanne is the one who just keeps going, going, and going." That is, until I stopped.

While people may think I never rest, in fact I've put many steps in place to ensure that I do. I go to bed early to enjoy some quiet time, I intentionally unplug from my devices for twenty-four hours every week, and I hand over my phone to my husband during the two vacations or so we take a year. Every step protects my health, both spiritual and physical. From working in a newsroom I have learned that these steps are crucial in order to lead well. The people who criticize you for resting likely fail to set and keep their own boundaries. To be alert and ready to answer God's call for your life, you need to rest.

Lessons Learned as a Child about the Sabbath

I recall that our parents did not allow us to do a variety of things on Sundays, such as mowing the lawn, because it was the "Lord's Day." They still refer to Sunday this way. Just this week my mom texted me wishing us a good "Lord's Day." Of course, every day is the "Lord's Day." She's describing the sacredness of the Sabbath— a day dedicated to worshipping God first before the distractions of the week engulf us. As a child, we met for worship twice on Sundays, morning and evening.

Our parents also took 1 Corinthians 16:1–2 very seriously: "Now about the collection for the Lord's people: Do what I told the Galatian churches to do. On the first day of every week, each one of you should set aside a sum of money in keeping with your income, saving it up, so that when I come no collections will have to be made" (NIV). They set an example by prioritizing giving. Even when things were tight, my dad wrote a perfectly folded check every week. He put it on top of the bookshelf in our family room so he wouldn't forget to pick it up on Sunday morning. In doing so, he taught me that giving and going to church were habits you needed to develop.

Less clear was how we fulfilled the command to rest on the Sabbath, for our Sabbath wasn't restful at all. I don't resent my parents or their jobs in ministry contributing to this lack of rest: it just was what it was. Sunday was our busiest, craziest day of the week. Between waking up early, being at church from early in the morning till the last people left for lunch, to attending church softball league games on Sunday afternoons, and being there every Sunday evening for worship, it was a day full of activity, not rest.

What I failed to understand as a child was that my dad rested on Mondays. True, he was always there when I arrived home from school on Mondays, and he monopolized the TV that day. But I never connected those dots until I worked in a newsroom and discovered how vital rest is—on whatever day you're able to take it.

Lessons Learned about Why God Created the Sabbath

Before I share the painful details of my newsroom crash that taught me about following God's command to rest, a word about how I learned why God created the Sabbath.

1. Our Sunday school teachers taught us that God rested on the seventh day: "By the seventh day God had finished the

work he had been doing; so on the seventh day he rested from all his work. Then God blessed the seventh day and made it holy, because on it he rested from all the work of creating that he had done" (Genesis 2:2–3, NIV).

2. Those same teachers told us of how God gave the Israelites a message about ensuring they rested: "Six days do your work, but on the seventh day do not work, so that your ox and your donkey may rest, and so that the slave born in your household and the foreigner among you may be refreshed" (Exodus 23:12, NIV).

3. Then God stated the need for rest as a command when he gave Moses The Ten Commandments: "Observe the Sabbath day by keeping it holy; as the LORD your God has commanded you ... but the seventh day is a Sabbath day of rest dedicated to the Lord your God, on which you must not do any work. This includes you, your sons and daughters, your male and female servants, your oxen and donkeys and other livestock, and any foreigners living among you. All your male and female servants must rest as you do." (Deuteronomy 5:12, 14, NLT).

4. Jesus reiterated the need to observe the Sabbath: "Then he said to them, 'The Sabbath was made for man, not man for the Sabbath.'" (Mark 2:27, NIV). If you can, stop and reread this verse out loud. What Jesus said is important to acknowledge. The Sabbath was made for *YOU*.

5. And in Colossians sits another verse about the importance of Sabbath keeping. It speaks directly to me and maybe also to you. It speaks to why you perhaps do not observe a Sabbath. It speaks to me because it addresses people who are more worried about what their bosses and coworkers might be thinking than about making sure they themselves carve out that weekly time to rest. "Therefore do not let anyone judge you by what you eat or drink, or with regard to a religious festival, a New Moon celebration

or a Sabbath day" (Colossians 2:16, NIV). You see, your insistence on rest may prompt people to question you. At those times, remember that you are called to be an example (Leviticus 20:26) and not to conform to the ways of this world (Romans 12:2). The ways of the world tell you to keep working. God's way is different. God created the Sabbath for you!

Lessons Learned about Why We Fail to Rest

Ironically, many of us find it hard to rest. Between growing work demands and the temptation to do things with and for your family (so you can put it up on social media to avoid feeling like a failure), we all struggle to prioritize the right things and slow down. It's become difficult to disconnect completely from everyone and everything else when our smartphones keep us permanently connected to our email, calendars, and social media accounts.

According to Demandsage, a data-gathering group that evaluates social media use, this is how usage lined up in 2023:

1. There are 4.9 billion social media users globally, meaning 60.49 percent of the global population use social media.

2. The global social media users are forecasted to reach 5.85 billion by 2027.

3. Facebook is the biggest social media platform, with 3.03 billion users.

4. The global social network penetration rate is 59.4 percent.

5. A typical social media user interacts with 6.6 social media platforms.

6. Social media is used by 85 percent of the world's 5.27 billion mobile phone users.

7. An average person uses social media for two hours and thirty-five minutes every day.

8. Millennials and Gen Z are the most frequent users of social media platforms.

The fastest-growing social network is TikTok, which has had a startling 105 percent user increase in the U.S. during the last two years.[53]

The reason I stopped resting was that I didn't turn things off—social media included. And I know I'm not alone. Nearly everyone struggles with it—including those in the church.

I know how hard it was for pastors and church leaders to disconnect, even before cell phones and email. Today it's even harder. So when I see churches and church plant organizations taking steps to ensure their leaders are getting a Sabbath, my inner child rejoices. Everyone is better for us re-filling our tanks.

When I think of the intentionality it takes to keep a Sabbath, I think of a former president of a media company for whom I worked. She's active on social media, but not only to post about work stuff. Some people may think that conveys she's distracted, doesn't have the right priorities, is unprofessional. In fact, she works extremely hard. Her days were long when we worked together, and she always got things done. But she rested when it was her turn to rest. And from those family posts on social media, I know her daughters are important to her and that she made it a priority to spend time with them.

She modeled the importance of being present wherever she was. When she was at work, she was at work. When she was with her family and friends, she was with them. She had balance in her life.

Still struggling with how to make rest happen? Here are a few ideas to help you "turn it off" so you can rest:

1. **Plan for rest.** I plan for my Sabbath. I have a teenage son who has activities. We serve at church. We have family. And my husband and I both work in news. So I have to be extremely intentional about getting my Sabbath on my calendar.

2. **Verbalize your rest.** I tell my boss, my husband and son, and my team when I am going to take time to rest so everyone has appropriate expectations for that time.

[53] Shubham Singh, "How Many People Use Social Media," Demandsage, September 2, 2024, https://www.demandsage.com/social-media-users/.

3. **Put the devices away.** You can have device-free zones, hours, or days. On the days when I plan to do this for a longer-than-usual period of time, I make sure my boss and other key people know how to reach Michael in case there is an emergency. In all my years of doing this, nobody has ever called Michael's cell phone to reach me. I may be important—and I am to some—but I'm not *that* important. Besides, my team is resourceful in my absence, and most things can wait until I return. Publicly establishing device-free times conveys to others that any interruptions had better be really important.

4. **Set the example.** I ensure that I am enabling people who report to me to rest. They make sure I rest as well.

5. **Trust others.** Trust those you have trained to lead and make decisions. Trusting others is at the core of turning work off. That may be one of the hardest steps to take because you have to trust.

Yet the payoff is real. When you are rested:

1. **You can give more.**

2. **You stay in the right frame of mind** for yourself and everyone around you.

3. **You will likely find you can do more with less time and are rejuvenated** after you have obeyed the command to rest.

4. You will have more peace.

Dear church, we haven't always helped ourselves or others to rest. We tend to glorify busyness. We make people feel guilty for resting, pushing them to fill their calendars with our church activities. No wonder they crash.

Lessons Learned from Crashing

In a matter of a few days in mid-March of 2020, we moved 90 percent of my staff of about 130 to a remote-style workforce (as perhaps your company did to you too). At the time, the majority of the news industry thought full remote newsrooms were not possible when we are producing live television every day. Yes, face-to-face communication in a deadline-driven culture is optimal, but we figured out within days that working remotely as a team was indeed possible.

Basically, every position except for anchors, a few producers, directors, and engineering positions were made remote. (Fortunately, our station had separate studios so we anchors could remain socially distanced.) Our editors edited from home. Editorial meetings were held remotely. Producers were producing from home. Our reporters and photographers did not come into the station as they had previously. Our assignment editors answered station phones and listened to scanners from home. It worked. If you'd seen saw how it all flowed together, you'd probably have thought, "Yay! They figured out how to address the work-life balance issue that news has faced for decades."

But not everyone thought we'd gotten it right. While work-life balance for some people became better, for others it became worse. Many of us ended up working *more* than we had before. Their commute time ended up being work time because it was now impossible to turn work off, so work continued. The only way to keep affected team members from melting down completely was a mandated sabbath.

We didn't call it a sabbath, of course. Instead we called it "unplug days." With the support of my boss, we made every manager take an "unplug day" every two weeks. My boss even made me, the leader of the newsroom, take an "unplug day." Other staff members' schedules were changed to four-day weeks to make sure they had extra unplug days to help them cope with all the stress we were under at the time.

It seemed like a perfect plan for everyone. But I didn't actually take my unplug days, even though I said I was taking them. I tried, but over time I'd check in more and more because I found it difficult to avoid being "on"—as I convinced myself, to avoid leading—through major events like racial injustice protests, riots, devastating tornadoes, and election controversy, as well as the turmoil of the pandemic.

Consequently, I rested less and less, even though I knew what I ought to do. I had mastered "unplug days" during my second major cancer fight. I religiously took twenty-four hours every week to refill my tank. But now I couldn't do it efficiently. I got to December of 2020 and realized I had spent nine months telling others to take time to rest without doing so myself. Instead, I let the pandemic send me spiraling toward every bad stress behavior in my repertoire. I was quick to become emotional, my eating was out of control, I was procrastinating, I wasn't delegating, and I was way too direct in my communication.

In short, I was taking care of others, but I wasn't taking care of myself at all. How well-intentioned my boss, my staff, or my husband were didn't matter, for when it comes down to it I'm the only one who can take care of myself. I am the only one who can decide if I am going to rest or not. I had decided I couldn't afford to take care of myself, and eventually it all caught up to me.

One Friday night that December I got a text from someone to whom I reported in our company asking me to come and talk about something the following week. Because I was exhausted, I reacted emotionally. I was over everything. The entire year had done me in. The caller couldn't have known because I'd never let on just how exhausted I was. I had hit bottom, and I desperately needed a break.

Thankfully, God had a plan for me. A year earlier, I had decided to write this book, but the news year of 2020 made it difficult to make any progress. I was depleted and for months had done nothing about filling my tank. In the middle of a night when I couldn't sleep because of that text from a superior, I wrote a letter to a Christian author, who had been having a lot of impact on women in the church, telling her about my life and what I wanted to do to help other women. Her assistant quickly made a referral to connect with the author's content consultant, who had helped get her manuscript ready for publication. Within a week, I was on my way to filling my tank again.

The year 2021 was no less stressful in the newsroom where I work, but I was in a better place because I was finally being more consistent in taking care of myself. That included starting my day with God. To end the day right, I knew I had to start the day right. I began to write more consistently, spent time with friends, and looked at my phone less. Even amidst challenges, I prioritized having a Sabbath.

God created the Sabbath for us, for you. It's up to you to take it. You are the only person who can ensure you are taking care of the heart, body, and mind that God gave you. Remember that your identity is in God, not in what you do or in what others think of you. So take the time to rest.

Lessons Learned about Having to Trust to Rest

Before it was trendy, I started choosing a "word" for the year. My "word" for 2021 was *trust*. When I heard that word, I was meditating and spending time in prayer focused on trusting God to show me his will for my life. Despite having heard the call years ago to go into news for a living, I now felt nudged to devote more time to empowering women to lead. Through all of 2019 and 2020, I felt the push to merge what I had learned up to that point of my life with this new direction to serve other women.

What I learned over the course of that year was about so much more than that. Yes, it was about trusting that God would show me his will and discovering that sometimes that would require me to take some big leaps out of my comfort zone. It was also about remembering to trust myself and to know that my identity is in God, not in what others think of me. More than anything, it was about learning to *trust others*. Trusting others is easier said than done because we can't control what others do. We can pray. We can influence. But at the end of the day, what they do is up to them.

Sometime during that year, I recall having a meeting with newsroom leaders about why some colleagues weren't stepping up. We wrestled with questions like "Why aren't they making decisions on their own?" and "Why are they always looking to us for guidance?" For years we had been talking about empowerment and trusting our people. So we were puzzled why they weren't they doing things on their own yet. I was really confused. I assumed that people wanted to be empowered and not micromanaged. I was puzzled by what I perceived as a lack of decision-making in day-to-day news coverage and a lack of initiative to make even simple news coverage plans.

Then a manager who reports to me and heard my frustration was brave enough to tell me, "Suzanne, it's one thing to say you trust. It's another thing to show it."

Whoa. For a moment I thought, "You do realize I hired you and that I can fire you if you're not going to support me?" Fortunately, that thought quickly dissipated, and I realized, "That is precisely why I hired this guy." He was right. Trust is an action verb. Building your people requires trusting them. Without that, they can't grow.

In a news organization trust can evaporate in a matter of seconds. Conveying incorrect information, a spelling error, a news reporter saying something when they thought a microphone was off, or showing bias in a story, for example, can wipe out any trust you have built with your viewers. And you may never get it back. When a mistake can erode all your hard work, trusting people to learn and make decisions is a really hard thing to do. It's particularly hard when public safety and reputations are at stake and when a misstep or error could ruin someone's life—including our own.

The only answer is to pick learning opportunities strategically and invest time in training. Through such caring and training, people do learn. You develop a relationship. They feel loved. And the mutual trust you build benefits everyone. On the one hand, the person you are growing and mentoring feels valued and follows the training. On the other, you as the mentor can breathe a bit easier because not everything is landing on you anymore. At all levels, your organization has to endorse such a culture, otherwise people feel paralyzed and unable to do anything without the approval of their boss. That is exhausting and it stifles trust.

Pastors and church leaders struggle with trust, too. There's a lot at stake: One indiscretion can result in people not trusting the church, its leaders, its members, and even the message. One instance of gossip. One misstep in a marriage. One misuse of funds.

Friends, the only way leaders can lead from a healthy place is not to be the only ones leading. Leaders have to build up others and trust them. That is the only way they will find rest. So if you're a leader, trust others to keep the train moving while you step away.

We find that hard to do because we all want to feel needed. We want to get the job done right. But consider Jesus' example: He trusted the disciples. He taught them in anticipation of the day he when he would no longer be physically present with them. God calls us to do the very same thing: to teach, to empower, and at some point to ask someone else to take the lead.

When I moved back to Atlanta to be the news director for WSB, I was invited to attend a dinner with some coworkers. During that dinner I sat next to a woman named Donna who had climbed through the ranks of my media company over the decades. She's a woman of faith, and I've always admired her wisdom. Our company and the station were about to undergo major changes to ownership and workflow. She no longer worked in my division but fully understood what I faced. I felt the call to lead my coworkers through the changes, but I knew it was going to be the hardest job I had ever accepted. Indeed, the others told me as much. New owners, new missions, and changing our workflows were all ahead. I was committed to working hard to project positivity and an "it will be okay" attitude. Nonetheless, I was open to getting as much wisdom as I could from others about how best to approach the changes.

Without even telling her, Donna knew what I was feeling and facing. She looked right at me and said: "You are about to go through a lot. You are going to be the rock for your staff, and your staff will need you. But you need a person too. Find that person to whom you can turn. You have to have that person."

She was right. Like Jesus, I did need someone to be my sounding board and to prop me up when I had tough moments. Friends, find your person or people. Find folks you trust. If sharing those moments with your spouse is too stressful for your or them, find someone else. Only be sure it's someone who won't compromise your marriage. You need people.

While it was certainly vital to have a trustworthy person to whom I could turn, my number one person wasn't a person at all: it was our Father in heaven, who invites us to bring all of our burdens to him and to trust him (1 Peter 5:7).

Before you can trust yourself or anyone else, you must trust God, as Proverbs 3:5–6 reminds us: "Trust in the LORD with all your heart, and lean not on your own understanding; in all your ways acknowledge him, and He shall direct your paths" (NKJV).

Like me, you'll find that when you trust him, you'll know how to empower and inspire others. You'll be able to trust those around you. You'll be able to loosen your tight grip and let others grow. Then you'll enjoy true rest.

ACTION ITEMS

1. If you are a church leader, then lead by example. Take your Sabbath and make sure your leadership team, staff, and volunteers are doing the same. Make sure your church's culture, programming, and messaging support this mandate.

2. Annually, in meetings and from the pulpit, teach your staff and your people about the Sabbath.

3. If you are a leader, study the Sabbath. When you understand the reasons for it, it's easier to make it happen.

4. Partner with a coach or trusted leader to map out how you can make Sabbath happen in your life in an ongoing way.

Self-Reflection Questions for Church Leaders

1. What systems do you need to create to ensure that your leaders, volunteers, and members can observe a Sabbath?

2. Which members of your congregation can you hold up as modeling the benefits of taking a Sabbath?

3. Does you church have counselors, programs, or people available for when someone "crashes"?

Self-Reflection Questions for Female Leaders

1. When was the last time you experienced real rest?

2. Whom can you trust to hold you accountable about taking a regular Sabbath?

3. Who is your person?

4. How might you help those you lead to be able to take a Sabbath?

5. What are the signs that indicate you need rest? What inhibits you from taking a Sabbath, and how can you remove those inhibitions?

13

Care for Others

The marketplace, businesses, and social media are filling the vacuum of caring that the church is leaving. It wasn't always that way. Growing up in the church I learned how to make food for food trains, visit the elderly, all of those check-the-box church things that "good Christians" do. I love doing those things and more. I believe in loving your neighbor, and I really missed the in-person community church stuff during the pandemic. Small groups have fostered a sense of community, especially in the mega-church world where that sense of knowing and taking care of people can be fostered. But it was in the newsroom that I felt true investment from my leaders and learned the value of self-growth, relationships, and comforting others. It was also in the newsroom that I learned it's okay to talk about mental health.

Lessons Learned about Self-Growth

My marketplace experience likely does not mirror yours. I have felt valued and had leaders who invested in me. My thirty-plus years in media, much of that for a single company, have been a time of immense growth and have given me a great sense of purpose.

I'm confident God was at work when I received a phone call in Fort Myers, Florida. I was about to get married, and my contract working as a line producer for a station in Fort Myers was coming to an end. I wanted to move to a larger market, and there was a position conveniently close in Orlando. The woman on the other end of the line was the executive producer for the top station in Orlando. She said my resumé had caught her attention because I had attended Milligan College (now University). She had grown up in the same church circles as I had and had friends who had attended Milligan.

During the course of our conversation, she outlined a number of reasons I should come and work for the Orlando station. One of the most compelling reasons she offered was that it was owned by one of the remaining "good TV groups" out there—good because they invested heavily in their people and good because they expected excellence. We were disciples of Jim Collins' book *Good to Great*. People in the business still today quote lines from it. Anything but first place was not accepted. But what that family-owned TV company did in return was treat people well. Not only did we receive amazing benefits, including a pension, but the company invested in us personally if we worked hard and showed potential. Between leadership training programs and one-on-one mentorship, we prided ourselves as being a company built on relationships—and on a bonus structure that rewarded loyalty. We were proud to work hard because we knew we'd be treated well in return.

Seeing my determination, work ethic, and commitment, my bosses designated me as a high-potential person early on. That led to programs, evaluations, coaches, and other unique opportunities. Let me be clear: While my bosses gave me a great deal, I gave a great deal, too. I worked long hours, and I was dedicated. I moved my family five times, once even to a city that I had never visited prior to taking the job. It was challenging, but I was rewarded, perhaps even favored. It was more than being in the right place at the right time—as I say, I worked really hard—and I wasn't the only one who received the same level of investment.

I did not receive such investment from the church until I reached my forties. That's when I had lunch with my friend and pastor's wife, Janie, while recovering from my third surgery after my breast cancer diagnosis. My cancer diagnoses gave me time to think. I felt a calling to lead women, and I needed to make sense of that with someone. Before my lunch with Janie, I literally got on my knees and prayed:

"God, I am ready to do something big for you. If something is to come out of this lunch, be big and bold." And was he ever!

It was during that meeting that Janie asked me to be in the first female discipleship group of her church planting organization. That was 2019. That group made a difference in the lives of all those women, including me.

As we focused on loving God with our heart, soul, and mind, the group discussed things that I had already learned in the marketplace, like identifying personality traits and stress triggers, how to have difficult conversations, and how to take care of oneself physically. It was great to hear these things from a spiritual perspective, and I was able to take those lessons and apply them to what I already knew about myself. For example, one lesson reminds us that Jesus led by surrounding himself with disciples, pushing the message to them, then leaving it up to them to get the message out. Jesus delegated.

As I made those connections, now well into my career, I couldn't help but think: *Wouldn't it have been awesome if I had learned those lessons from the church when I was a woman in my twenties?* Maybe if I had learned earlier this biblical example of leading by taking care of my people, like Jesus fed his followers and earned their trust, I wouldn't have reacted to people and situations with such strong emotion. And perhaps if I had connected my personality assessments to the thinking that God made me as uniquely me, I could have slowed down and exhaled a bit more. Maybe I would have been more patient and caring toward a colleague who was not performing well on the job or whose job was being cut.

Instead of from the church, those lessons have come from people who think more about revenue, expense controls, employee turnover rates, and ratings than whether I love my neighbor, how I treat the least of these, or whether I am kind. If I had learned in the church to ask God for wisdom when pausing before I spoke, maybe my words would have been wiser. If I had learned in the church to think of others more than of myself, perhaps I would not have spiraled out of control and frustrated others.

Most of our churches do a fairly good job providing ministry programming through high school and even college. But what do we do for our young adults when they enter the workforce or finish college? How do we continue to form young adults in the faith and keep them in the church?

As so many people do, I fell away from my faith around my senior year in college and stayed away until my late twenties. Why does this happen so frequently? And what can we do to help young adults engage and grow in their faith?

A 2017 study conducted by Lifeway gives the top reasons church dropouts say they stopped attending church.[54] Moving from home tops the list, but the three other top reasons are the church's judgment, lack of connection, and stances on political and social issues. I get it. While I don't believe there are quick solutions, the church can do things like foster a sense of belonging and connection instead of assuming workplaces and other sources should or will do so. The Bible talks about this in Hebrews 5:12–14:

> Though by this time you ought to be teachers, you need someone to teach you the elementary truths of God's word all over again. You need milk, not solid food! Anyone who lives on milk, being still an infant, is not acquainted with the teaching about righteousness. But solid food is for the mature, who by constant use have trained themselves to distinguish good from evil (NIV).

Surely it is our job in the church to bridge the gap from milk to solid food. Surely we can convey to young adults that we believe in them by hosting coaching sessions, leadership groups, social events, and seminars on subjects directed to them. Let's be the ones to comfort and console them. Let's be the ones to listen to them and praise them. Let's help them discover who God made them to be. Defining or limiting their potential should not be left up to their employers.

---

[54] Lifeway Research, "Most Teenagers Drop Out of Church When They Become Young Adults," January 15, 2019, https://lifewayresearch.com/2019/01/15/most-teenagers-drop-out-of-church-as-young-adults/.

Lessons Learned about Comforting Others

Comfort is one thing all young adults need. That's been particularly true in these pandemic and post-pandemic years. People are exhausted, lonely, and sad. Yet whereas once the church was the go-to place for comfort and consolation, now all too often people perceive the church as divisive and unkind.

Jesus welcomed everyone. He loved everyone—even those he knew to be sinners. Recall the story of Zacchaeus in Luke 9:1–10. Or the story of the sheep and the goats in Matthew 25, in which Jesus tells us that whatever we do "for the least of these," we do for him. Surely the church is called to be the one place, above all others, where everyone should feel loved. To be loved means you feel welcomed. To be loved means having a shoulder to cry on. To be loved means being noticed.

It was this sense of feeling loved that drew me back to church and kept me there. After the passing of my aunt, who was an example of a strong business leader and Christian woman, I decided to return to my faith. I recall having felt very alone on Sunday mornings. That was until one such morning when I was running late and the older woman who greeted me at the door of the church smiled really widely and said, "Well, there you are!" She hugged me, and I went to my seat and cried because I felt welcomed again. I felt loved. The women in that church continued to love me as I became more comfortable and signed up for teaching, studies, and more. But what prompted all that was that one greeter recognizing me and welcoming me back with open arms.

If people aren't getting love and support from Christians and the church, where are they getting it? Every company for which I have worked has offered employee assistance programs to show care and provide opportunities for its employees' betterment and emotional well-being. This has included everything from counseling to child care assistance, from paying employees' bills during medical crises to weight loss programs.

One of the hardest times of managing a newsroom came while I was writing this book. Then in her early fifties, our long-term anchor,

Jovita Moore, was diagnosed with terminal brain cancer. While my boss and I were discussing with our corporate leaders, Marian and Paul, all the things we'd do for our staff the day we informed them of her diagnosis, Marian interrupted and said: "Lean on all of the technical and logistical assistance corporate can give you. Your job is to be here for your people."

She was right. Our jobs were to be there for our people. And, dear church, our job is also to be there for our people. That includes *everyone*, no matter what their sin looks like.

As a I child, I learned that a parable is "an earthly story with a heavenly meaning." That resonates with me when I think about the parable of the sheep and goats in which the king separates the two. It's in Matthew 25. Find your Bible, read this parable, and come back.

My pastor, Derek, recently spoke about this passage. The way he put it was new to me. I was familiar with the notion of being the hands and feet of Jesus. That's a tall order to fill. But this scripture talks about Jesus being in others. When we are kind and care for the "least" of our brothers and sisters, we are kind and caring toward Jesus. If you see Jesus in everyone, you see them in a different light.

Dear church, Jesus commanded us to comfort everyone. If we're not there for them, they'll go somewhere else. That somewhere else may be a place of addiction, idolatry, depression, and more. Duly cautioned, let's try again to be there for "the least of these."

Lessons Learned about Showing Up

Sometimes "being there" merely requires that you respond to a need. Don't wait for someone in need to ask because usually people are too overwhelmed, proud, or shy to seek out your help. Create a community through Zoom. Drop food off for someone who needs it without being asked. Offer a kind word. Stop and listen to what's bothering others. Meet people where their needs are. Instead of waiting for people to show up for church, let's be the church and show up for them every day in their community gyms, workplaces, schools, and neighborhoods.

Other people and business and bosses are showing up when people need them. They're organizing virtual get-togethers when they can't meet in person. They're organizing exercise clubs and pods. They're using technology to meet people where they are. So maybe we, the church, could learn a thing or two from them.

Each time I've fought cancer, my coworkers showed up for me as much as my church family did. That's *a lot* of people from both sides of my life. So how can the church stand out? Let's be a safe place where people can bring all of their concerns and feelings, confident they'll encounter love and understanding. Let's be genuine and bold about the grace and love that drive us.

Nowadays, people no longer have to depend on the church for connection, food, or care. Gone are the days in which the Church prayer chain was the primary way of sharing concerns. Nowadays we connect through neighborhood apps, social media sites, and quick, informal texts. Many people are replacing church connections with these other sources because they are finding more unconditional love and care in other organizations than they do inside our church walls.

Statistics back this up. A 2021 study by Pew Research showed the number of unaffiliated adults or "nones" (adults who don't identify with a religion) now applies to 29% of adults. In 2007, only 16% of adults considered themselves "nones." And while these "nones" have no religious identity, they are engaged in community somewhere because it's a basic human need. A 2017 study published in the American Journal of Lifestyle Medicine determined that community is critical for good health. The authors wrote:

> Social connection is a pillar of lifestyle medicine. Humans are wired to connect, and this connection affects our health. From psychological theories to recent research, there is significant evidence that social support and feeling connected can help people maintain a healthy body mass index, control blood sugars, improve cancer survival, decrease cardiovascular mortality, decrease depressive symptoms, mitigate posttraumatic stress disorder symptoms, and improve

overall mental health. The opposite of connection, social isolation, has a negative effect on health and can increase depressive symptoms as well as mortality.[55]

People find community, whether it be in the church or not.

I've seen many of them find community at work. The organization YPulse, which describes itself as the leader in marketing insights for Gen Z'ers and Millennials, published this data. Their research indicates people find community outside their circle of family and friends. They listed social media, video games, work, and interest groups above organized religion as sources of community among Millennials.[56]

Before my husband, Michael, became a believer, he gave me some good insights into how some non-believers may view churches as a source of community. While visiting my parents' small country church, he said, "I can see why people in small towns gravitate to churches for community and support." It made me think. Michael always found community through our jobs and the closeness we felt to our coworkers. Though it's true that we fill holes in our hearts with things or people of the world, what truly satisfies is God. You see, community tied to our job, fitness, or social media can become our ultimate concern—our god.

People are often attracted to such things because they need community and love. But if we aren't careful, we can confuse God's unconditional love for the empty or broken love of those with selfish desires. God instructed us to love one another, for when we love with God's love, we serve as his hands and feet and love each other as Jesus commanded us to do. That's community. That's a fulfilling community. In John 15:12–13 Jesus said: "My command is this: Love each other as I have loved you. Greater love has no one than this: to lay down one's life for one's friends" (NIV).

[55] Jessica Martino, Jennifer Pegg, and Elizabeth Pegg Frates, "The Connection Prescription: Using the Power of Social Interactions and the Deep Desire for Connectedness to Empower Health and Wellness," *American Journal of Lifestyle Medicine* 11, no. 6 (November-December 2017): abstract, https://www.ncbi.nlm.nih.gov/pmc/articles/PMC6125010/.

[56] YPulse, "These are the Top Places Gen Z & Millennials Say They Find Community," April 20, 2021, https://www.ypulse.com/article/2021/04/20/these-are-the-top-places-gen-z-millennials-say-they-find-community/.

That commandment is easier said than done. I mean, we can say we love each other and drop food off as part of a meal train. But are we loving and helping others who have started drinking too much during a pandemic? If we know they haven't left their home for months, have we bothered to check on them? Have we given our time and money, no questions asked? Or have we assumed someone else is doing whatever's necessary? Do we think it's the pastor's job? Jesus is asking us to lay down our lives for our friends every day. He's asking us to be selfless. He's asking us to think of others first when it comes to our time, money, and conveniences. That's love. That's true and fulfilling community.

Lessons We Can Share

One big thing I have learned about taking care of people is to be flexible. I have learned to meet others where they are. From whom did I learn this? From people at work. When people in the church were too busy to care for me when I was sick, people at work met me where I was by making my job accessible, by coaching me through new tasks, and of course by caring for me and my family.

Dear church, in order to be there for everyone, including "the least of these," we have to figure out who we are trying to reach and identify and overcome whatever unconscious biases we have to do so effectively. Let's examine our own sin. Do we turn a blind eye to our own shortcomings but so shine a spotlight on others' sin that we won't even associate with people who have different views than ours?

Living in a bubble and associating only with like-minded people is not bringing people into the church but alienating them. It's time to examine our behaviors and pivot. In the newsroom we call this being "nimble."

Dear church, we can be nimble and pivot without compromising our beliefs. Loving someone, forging a relationship with someone who disagrees with you, does not automatically lead you down the wrong path. But it may force you to examine not only some of your beliefs and sins but perhaps primarily your actions—or lack of them. And in doing so, perhaps you'll realize it's you who needs to make a shift.

My dad officiated at our wedding, and to the surprise of some he did so when Michael was still not a believer. Was he compromising his beliefs? As I've gotten older, I realize I put my dad in an awkward situation. I'm sure he lost sleep over it. But I've also grown to respect his wisdom. Apparently my dad realized that, to get me back on the right path, and for Michael to find the right path, he first had to have a solid relationship with us. Instead of alienating the two of us and making an already awkward relationship more so, he chose the path of love.

I'm proud to say that my parents never gave up on Michael. They prayed for him. They gave him Bibles and books for gifts. My mom held me accountable and once suggested to me that perhaps I didn't want Michael to become a Christian because he would likely be "all in" whereas back then I perhaps wasn't interested in living an "all in" life for Jesus. My parents made a pivot in the way they approached the situation. It worked.

I challenge you to think about how the places to which young adults are gravitating may more closely exemplify what being the hands of feet and Jesus looks like than your church does. Where have they turned because Christians are refusing to "pivot" and are therefore alienating those who need them most? We have this calling to love the lonely, the depressed, the hungry, the sick. We can't be choosy when it comes to whom to love. Like Jesus, we are being called to those in need, not only to those who think and look like us.

ACTION ITEMS

1. Create self-growth plans and opportunities for young men *and* women in your congregations.

2. If you are a young leader, create leadership opportunities and lead the effort to bring others into the church.

3. Evaluate the outreach programs your church is currently offering. Identify the people in your congregation who can run exercise programs and the like that can build community in the church.

4. Make a list of how your church is there for your community in ways others are not. If you can't find any, determine the ways you can be bold and stand out to draw people in need into your church family.

Self-Reflection Questions for Church Leaders

1. When and how has your church helped to develop young male leaders more than young female leaders?

2. How does your congregation show up for its members and your community?

3. Do the "least of these" feel loved by your church? Why or why not? If you answered no to the first question, what can you change?

Self-Reflection Questions for Female Leaders

1. What are you doing to ensure your personal growth?

2. How are you helping other women to grow?

3. How do you show up for others?

4. What have you done to ensure that the "least of these" feel loved by you?

SECTION 4

Be the Solution

14

Look Out for Other Women

Throughout much of my adult life, if you had told me I was not alone on Sunday mornings at church, I would not have believed you. Those three hours on Sunday were the loneliest three hours of my week. Here's why.

I mentioned in the previous chapter that I wasn't an angel in my early to mid-twenties and that it was my husband, Michael, who brought me around. I would not encourage you to emulate my path because it was rough one, full of pain. Though rough, that painful path opened my eyes to how the church typically treats the "untraditional believer."

Lessons Learned through Painful Experiences at Church

By "untraditional believer" I mean anyone besides the picture-perfect married couple with kids. While I understand that churches' family focus comes from a good place, such churches' structure, approach, and messaging can cause considerable pressure and alienation. Because churches' programs, sermons, and get-togethers tend to be family-focused, if you don't have a "family," it's hard to fit in. Even if we make those things more open to those who aren't part of a traditional family unit, for many people just showing up at church and seeing others being attended to as family units can be painful. I left many church events to sob in my car because I felt unloved and alienated by other believers. This caused me to question what grace really is and whether it is real, and it made me doubt that God loves me unconditionally.

So I was taken aback when I still felt like an outsider even after Michael became a believer, particularly because those who most made me feel like an outsider and a failure as a Christian woman were other women.

Perhaps some of those feelings were rooted in my calling and purpose being so different to many Christian women's callings—at least as I perceive them in many evangelical churches. In those circles, being a good Christian woman typically means keeping up with her duty to serve her husband and children first, to be responsible for the upkeep of their home, and to demonstrate how frugal she is. Women who work outside of the home or remotely for an employer have to signal that their job does not infringe on the above listed duties, lest they be perceived as having abdicated their chief roles as a wife, mother, and homemaker.

As soon as a woman co-teaching Sunday school with me discovered that I worked in news, she informed me that had been her dream but she couldn't imagine how to fulfill it and still be a Christian. I sat there, quietly stunned.

She then told me she feels blessed that her husband has been able to provide for their family so she doesn't have to work. I wanted to snap back, "This is *not* about God blessing *you* more than *me*, and I'm pretty sure my husband would make more than yours if he chose not to let his career take a backseat to mine." Yet I kept my mouth shut.

Even Christian women fall into a competitive mindset and tear each other down to justify themselves. I couldn't make her understand me, but I could try to understand her.

Lessons Learned in the Newsroom about Understanding Others

That advice from a coworker came when Price was less than a year old. When I gave birth to him, my husband was still working for a twenty-four-hour cable network, and I was an executive producer at a local station working overnight shifts because the newscast I oversaw was in the morning. The shift had some advantages: I participated in every school event and went to every one of Price's medical appointments, even if it meant I didn't sleep. Michael did overnight duty and took Price to the daycare across the street from where I worked. When I got off work around 9:00 a.m., I would stop at the daycare, talk to his teachers, nurse him, and spend about an hour with him. I'd then go home and sleep, and Michael would pick him up when his shift ended around 5:00 p.m. Then we'd have a few hours in the evening together. For the most part it worked. However, in my "I can do everything" mindset, I decided to be the daycare room mom.

This daycare wasn't the cheapest. It charged at the upper end of the scale, but it was close to our workplaces, I could stop by at a moment's notice, and the people there became like family to us. Surprisingly, some of these kids' moms didn't even work part time and tended to be intense helicopter moms. The parents' meetings and events were likewise intense. I quickly and unexpectedly discovered that there were written and unwritten rules of what constituted appropriate "mom" behavior regarding everything from the appropriate gifts to give the teachers to what you fed your child.

One week I was working during the day and told my supervising manager over lunch that I needed to run across the street to the daycare to help with decorations for an event. I mentioned I was not the decorating type and, quite frankly, that I did not feel as if I belonged in that group of moms. I felt like an outsider. She replied matter-of-factly, "Just remember they are as insecure around you as you are around them." That was what I needed to hear.

At about the same time, I was having a conversation with another female manager at the station because she had heard someone ask me whether I was planning to have another child. I assured her it wasn't in our plans at the time since Price was still an infant, and I noted it was hard enough to parent even one child on my schedule.

She graciously encouraged me: "As a working mom, your time with Price is not the same as a mom who is home with her kids all day. You will learn how to value the time you do have with him." In short, it's different, and that's okay. To this day, I remind myself of her words when I am with him.

And all these years later, my staff still understands that my special time with Price is at night. On occasion, executive producers have stopped staff members from calling me late at night, reminding them: "That is her special time with her son, so it had better be a big deal for you to call her right now."

That special time includes about an hour of talking with him and putting him to bed every night. I often fall asleep with him in the process. Up until the age of eleven, he would tell you that was our special time. When he was little I started verbalizing to him the importance of that time. No matter how much he heard me talk about work, I wanted him to know that time with him was more precious to me than work. I'd ask, "What is the best part of my day?" and when he was little, he'd ask me the same question and I'd reply, "Right now." These days when I ask my teenaged son, "What's the best part of my day?," he still replies, "Right now."

Lessons Learned about Asking for Help

From women at work I learned that it's okay to ask for help. From how to dress to cleaning my house, I have certainly received a lot of help over the years. I've noticed that a big difference between marketplace women and women in the church is that women in the marketplace are a bit more comfortable asking for, accepting, and offering help. In my church circles it seems as if women are expected to love their home duties. Those are a source of pride and identity. Their husbands brag about it, and over time the traditional gender roles have fed a perception that women naturally thrive in certain domains. Unfortunately, this creates pressure and a lack of authenticity among many women in the church.

My company, which has historically had significant female executive leadership, dedicated an entire month to women talking to women about everything from cleaning to managing child care to breaking the glass ceiling. It organized webinars and embedded videos on the company's website to create awareness and advocate for health in those areas. It also posted articles written by women sharing how they do life. I'm not sure whose idea it was, but it was clear that the female executive leaders in the company embraced sharing what they had learned over time.

The piece of advice that most struck me most was not to do everything on your own. That advice giver was right: If you can afford it, hire someone to clean your toilets. To quote my late Aunt Carol, who was one of the first professional women I knew: "There is something you can sacrifice to get the time back you'd spend cleaning your house." For me and many others, she's right: There is something worth sacrificing for a maid service. We may not stay in the best rooms or hotels when we travel. We don't trade cars very often. We are slow to remodel our house. Those are things I don't do but could justify doing with my income. I sacrifice on those things to ensure I can give generously to others and the church and can still afford to pay for help when I need it. I look at it as a win-win. Price doesn't know he's staying in a less expensive hotel; he's happy to be with me and Michael. And he gets to spend more weekend time with us because we use the money we've saved to pay someone to help around the house.

Moreover, if you are a high wage-earning woman, hiring people to do some things like cleaning your house can be a blessing, because it gives you the chance to be an employer. And you know what? I believe as a female leader in my day job and at home that hiring out for some things provides me with opportunities to serve others.

During the COVID-19 pandemic I was blessed that my income did not take the nosedive many others experienced. Our giving remained the same. And early on, when we could not let the people who clean our house come inside for three months, I still paid them. For me, it was an act of service to continue paying them. They wrote and explained that my family's generosity was the reason they had been able to pay their rent. They know what I do for a living. They clean my house. They see my calendar. They know what books I read. They know I call myself a Christian. And I hope and pray that the young couple sees Christ's love in the way I treat them in my house once a week, as much as the people who work for me full time in a newsroom.

Lessons Learned about Being There at All Times

How and why did I learn more lessons from women in the marketplace than in the church? It's not unusual for career women to find camaraderie and support at work rather than at church. I believe this is largely because for centuries churches typically promoted gender-based rather than gift-based family roles. Now that we are at a transition point, it's time for the church to acknowledge this and correct it.

It was only in my mid-forties that I found women at church who helped me to navigate the balance of my work and my faith in any objective way. Until then, my "figure it outers" were women at work. Advice from Christian women might have meant even more to me and gone deeper. For example, that advice might have gone a step further and suggested that I focus on praying for the other women who behaved insensitively to me, instead of focusing only on my feelings about their behavior. And how awesome it would have been if the conversation about valuing the time I do have with Price had gone further and imagined how I might form him in his faith. Imagine the ripple effect those conversations could have had in my life, in my son's life, and in the kingdom!

One of the biggest obstacles I had with my spiritual growth as a professional woman were my hours. I wanted to take part in every Beth Moore and Lysa TerKeurst Bible study my church offered, but they typically took place in the daytime, preventing working women like me from attending. Classes offered in the evening took place so early that I couldn't make it in time for those either. Dear church, we can care for other women by making our programs for women more accessible.

We can also care for working women by making ourselves available. When I'm leaving the office at 7:30 p.m. on a weeknight, if I need to talk out my problems over dinner, I can name ten women in my professional circles who would drop everything and do it. They would give me lots of good advice and care, albeit none of it prayed over, much of it not based in scripture.

In contrast, at 7:30 p.m. on any given weeknight my church circle friends are not as available. Those are the women from whom I need to hear about the problems I'm facing. Those are the women from whom working Christian women in general need to hear. Dear church women, make yourselves available. Create caring circles for and with others! Dear churches, community pastors, and women's ministry leaders, examine your existing programs and services and ask yourselves whether you have something to meet the needs of everyone in your congregation. If you are unsure whether you are already meeting the needs of your congregation, ask women if they feel included. If they answer no, ask them what it would take for them to feel included and consider making adjustments.

As Price grew older and my faith grew stronger, I did seek out ways to make sure I was included. In my next city and church, I found a time slot for Bible study and small groups that worked for my job, even though it was with a group of women who were all over sixty. At first I was disappointed thinking I'd have nothing in common with them at this earlier stage of my life, but it was one of the most faith-building experiences for me. I remember seeing the description of the study in the bulletin and asking a friend of my age whether she thought I'd like it. She told me who was in the group, and despite my hesitance she encouraged me: "Suzanne, I think they would speak so much life into you, and you would do the same for them."

I don't know if that friend has the spiritual gift of prophecy, but what she said to me that day was definitely prophetic. The leader is a gifted and wise teacher, and the women shared awesome stories of great faith. The prayer time was also rich, and the women supported each other in ways I hadn't experienced prior to joining that group. I never once felt judged for being a working mom in the media. They even prayed for my husband's salvation with me. When Michael accepted Jesus (within months of my joining that group), they cheered. On the day he was baptized, they ended their class early to come into the sanctuary and celebrate his baptism.

I coveted my experiences in that group. The group changed me, and it changed my perspective of women in the church and what it should look like to be in community together. Unfortunately, I stopped meeting with that group when Michael started coming to church with me because we attended the service that took place when they were meeting. Sitting with him at the service had to be my new priority during that season. And eventually my options to coordinate my day job, attend a service with my family, and go to a study where I could grow again became limited.

I have connected with a few other all-female church groups in the years since then, and I've taken a great deal from those experiences. I felt loved and supported, but I recognize those experiences are rare for many working women. That's unfortunate. In my opinion we are the women who need the mentoring the most to be able to go out into the marketplace and be the light of Christ. Imagine if women in the church paused and realized we're all struggling at times and that we all need a friend. Imagine if women stopped to ask how they could reach those women—the women like me. Perhaps then we would truly be "carrying each other's burdens" as Paul teaches us in Galatians 6:2. Here's the thing: I know there were other women in and beyond those churches who would have benefited from that kind of care. How must we change to draw them into our circles?

Lessons Learned about Finding Your Circle

My dominant strength in *Strengthfinder* is competition. If I can't win, I won't play. And while I'm super good at being competitive, I know I'm not alone in this. We women have a tendency toward competition and judgment. It's what keeps us from helping each other grow—that is, until we find women like ourselves.

It is no coincidence that when Michael and I moved to another city, our new church was one that embraced women in leadership. It was the same church in which I found that group of professional women I mentioned earlier. The leader of that women's group was a "lead team" member, or what some would call an elder in the congregation. I believe I gravitated to that group knowing it was filled with leading ladies with whom I could share experiences and a Christian perspective.

However, I had to do double small group duty to be part of it. You see, I wanted to be part of a small group with my husband, too. Michael needed to grow in faith, and I felt it was important for our marriage to attend a group together. Besides, I had spent the previous fifteen years being lonely in small groups thinking about how awesome it would be if he were there. Now that I had a husband willing to attend one, I needed to be there with him.

Meanwhile, I approached our community formation pastor about wanting to lead a group for professional women, and he suggested I participate in an existing women's group. I signed up, and it was awesome! The leader was a single pharmaceutical sales rep who is an amazing leader. Some of the women were single, and some were married with spouses in the church who just wanted female fellowship. Some also worked during the day. Some were new moms, and some were grandmas. We women were a mixed bag of backgrounds and experiences with a shared faith, and those women were there when I needed them. They surprised me with a huge dinner party before my double mastectomy. They let me host them when I was undergoing cancer treatment and felt the need to entertain, even though I wasn't at my best. I just needed to have company without feeling like I was a cancer patient. They also showered me with flowers, gifts, coffee, visits, cupcakes, meals—whatever I needed. They even helped me decorate my house for Christmas. That is what I needed. And that is what other women need, too.

I was fortunate. I know many working women who never receive that kind of support in our churches. Why?

First, we're all stretched thin. It's hard to give support at the drop of a hat. And for many of us women it's hard to be vulnerable and admit to other women that we need help. Not only do we have our families and jobs, but we are also working to grow our faith. That takes time, too. Unless we find a circle of people to help us find ways to make that time, it won't happen. We women need to do our part seeking out our people. It's an investment of time and emotional energy. And if we don't invest, we won't experience the depth needed to allow others to jump into our trenches with us.

Dear church, let's seek out whoever is falling between the cracks. Jesus didn't overlook or overstep anyone. He went out of his way and invested time and energy into people who were all around him. Our calling is to do the same, even if it takes some hard work.

Second, working women often are not the target audience of our churches. Most churches focus on reaching the traditional family unit. That traditional family may or may not include a working woman. And when churches' financial and volunteer resources are strained, what you need as a single, working woman may not be the top priority of their programming or outreach. That's why it's important for those of you who are now aware of this gap to step up and serve in areas where we can form women in the faith.

When Price was little, I volunteered to lead a "moms of little ones" group. We weren't many in number. But we met regularly, at 8:30 p.m. It was specifically at that time so we could get our children to bed first before jetting off to Starbucks for coffee together. While the time probably wasn't ideal for some of the moms, it was for me and a few others who really needed the outlet and fellowship, so we made it happen. It made me realize that if you need something, others probably do too, so you should step up and be part of the solution.

Third, stop using your competitive spirit to compare yourself to each other. While it's easy to do because social media presents the highlight reels in each other's lives, the vice of comparison has had a long shelf life—even back to Jesus' time.

Remember the sisters Mary and Martha? Martha was a bit judgy. And she spoke up about it. While it's easy to judge Martha, as someone who can identify with Martha I can confidently tell you she was exhausted! She was constantly having to pull her weight. But I also recognize she was thinking mostly about *herself* and what *she* was doing.

Whoops! And we're back to that humility thing again. When we humble ourselves, we can be there for others. We humble ourselves by realizing we're not going to find our circle by sitting around waiting for it to find us. It takes time, energy, vulnerability, and even a little elbow grease. But that work is well worth it. God wants you to have your circle. He wants you to be surrounded by like-minded women with whom you can identify, struggle, laugh, and cry. Put some work into finding such people and you will find your circle. Not only will it help you, but it will refocus your eyes to helping those around you.

Lessons Learned about Being Better Together

I look back at the times in my adult life when the circle of which I was part was not made up of fellow Christians. Those times were lonely. I made decisions and behaved in ways that scripture did not support. But I did learn how important it is for women to support women. I learned that we are better together.

Women, it's time. It's time for us to rise up and get over our insecurities. It's time to stand on the solid ground of knowing we are all loved and uniquely gifted to do amazing things. We can be the ones who spark change. We can show what it means to love God with every ounce of our being and to love our neighbor as ourselves.

Such change and love take strength. They take courage. But I know we are up to the task. I know we can do it when we support each other. I pray that leading women who are Christians find that support with women who share their faith, and I pray they will mentor women who are coming up behind them. Perhaps you are one such leading woman. When we get over our differences and look at each other as sisters, all equally loved by God, we will grow and advance his kingdom. And we will live on earth as in heaven. What a day that will be!

ACTION ITEMS

1. Examine what programs are available to the women in your church, and make sure they are designed for *all* of them.

2. Make a list of people who can step up and lead non-traditional groups at non-traditional times in your congregation.

3. Make a point of introducing people who have similar family dynamics to one another.

4. Ask for feedback after family and church events. The marketplace does this well. Churches hear from the noisy folks. Churches would get more valuable feedback if they consistently asked for feedback as businesses do.

Self-Reflection Questions for Church Leaders

1. Whom have you unknowingly alienated while trying to reach your "target audience"? What can you do to welcome those people back into your church family?

2. Who in your congregation can help you to think "outside the box" when it comes to creating small groups and mentorships?

3. What dialogue have you enabled that suggests that certain families have a more "blessed" path than others?

Self-Reflection Questions for Female Leaders

1. How can you help support female leadership in your church?

2. How have you spoken up when you felt alienated or when you saw a circumstance that could potentially alienate others?

3. From whom can you learn what you are not taking the time to see?

4. How are you supporting those who have supported you?

15

Pave the Way

I started this book by saying it was not my goal to change your mind about the role of women in leadership. Either your mind is made up, or you are currently working that out with God. I brought that up at the very beginning because no matter where you are—a complementarian, egalitarian, or feminist—I didn't want to alienate you. The messages and stories you've read here are ones I believe I'm supposed to share with everyone. And I believe they can be applied to everyone, no matter your beliefs on this matter. But I do encourage you to fact-check your Jesus about women and all the issues we've tackled throughout this book. Journalists fact-check information every day. You must do the same. In doing so, you may find that what are you doing every day does not line up with what you actually believe—especially when it comes to women's roles at home and in the church.

My goals for this book were to discuss how we, the church, can better embrace and support young girls and women who are wired to lead and to examine how well we, the church, serve *everyone*. Some of the lessons I address in this book I learned in a newsroom, not necessarily because the church doesn't address those issues, but because I was a young woman and wasn't included in the circles in which they were discussed. But other lessons I learned in local newsrooms because those newsrooms exposed me to people, problems, and solutions from which the church actually sheltered me, whether consciously or not.

You may say, "Suzanne, clearly God's plan was for you lead in newsrooms." That's true of my path, but I believe it disregards the bigger issue for other women and the church as a whole. I know God has a unique plan for each of us and his plan won't be thwarted by the limits placed on us by humans. We see throughout scripture that God's omnipotence reigns for his people, even in the most unlikely situations. God is big, and he sees the whole picture of our lives. Neither the limitations we place on ourselves nor those placed on us by small theology or the biases of our culture can change the trajectory of God's ultimate good for us. But we can partner with him in making it easier for the next generation. That is what I dream about for the church. This is what this book has been about. And that is why I believe it was God's plan that I write this book.

Many people in my generation and the ones before mine came to faith and returned to the church after they had had kids and were a bit older. Merely to assume that the faith we teach our children will move to their hearts as they become older is a gamble we should not take. In fact, a 2019 Pew Research study found that four in ten teenagers only "do religious things" because their parents want them to.[57] In other words, their faith is not their own.

Time brings change, and unfortunately many of the changes we see in our culture continue to widen the gap between a love for God's house and indifference toward the "antiquated" faith of our church fathers. Yes, it's our job as parents to raise our children with a foundation for their faith by talking about spiritual matters, helping them see the world through a biblical worldview, and making church engagement a priority of our households. But if we don't encourage our children to explore the tenets of the faith for themselves, down the road that foundation may develop some serious cracks in it. Then, when the church fails to embrace them because they are a female with leadership skills that aren't welcome or because that particular church does not have programming for them as young adults, where will they turn? Where will they go when they are exploring their autonomy,

---

[57] "U.S. Teen Take After Their Parents Religiously, Attend Services Together and Enjoy Family Rituals," *Pew Research Center,* September 10, 2020, https://www. pewforum.org/2020/09/10/what-do-parents-want-for-their-teens/.

starting to make sense of the world around them, and forming their values and identities?

Yes, it's our job as parents to raise our children with a foundation. But if we don't ensure our children's faith is their own, and if the church doesn't embrace each child's whole self, where will our children turn as young adults?

Lessons I've Shared with You

Throughout this book I've shared lessons I learned while working in newsrooms across the country. They are lessons I had hoped to learn in our churches. Instead, I learned them in the workplace.

I learned about justice and ethics in a newsroom. We have biases that are deeply rooted—sometimes in sin. We have to follow Jesus' lead and address those biases. When we do that, we can truly love our neighbors and are not intimidated by doing the right thing. Doing so also enables us to speak truth to our brothers and sisters in love. If we don't first address the justice and ethics issues to which the church has turned a blind eye, we can't take those other steps.

I learned about how to handle gender issues by working in a newsroom. There, I learned to regard others based on their God-given gifts, not primarily based on their gender. This includes understanding why some men with good intentions unknowingly hold back and diminish their sisters in Christ. It includes knowing that the Spirit guides me through tough situations and conversations simply because he is always there and always helping us walk in the ways of God. Sin happens when we don't listen to the Spirit. When we don't listen, we tend to give in to our baser instincts, including but not only sexual ones. The free will God gave us he expects us to use to increase his glory here on earth.

It was in a newsroom that I learned how women can support women. I learned to stand up for myself and not let others push me in directions that fulfill their dreams for me, not mine. I learned that it's up to God and me to determine his plan for me, not someone else. And I learned that through it all I am not alone. And neither are you. When women get out of each other's way and help each other, they do great things.

I've also learned that I've got to take care of myself in order to grow, and to help others to do the same. God is the only one I need please, not others. Such growth depends on setting and keeping boundaries and taking care of myself, especially by taking a sabbath regularly. It's only then that I have the wherewithal to take care of others and to be a good wife, mom, boss, and follower of Jesus.

Where Do We Go from Here?

The debate over our roles and how God intended them to be is not a new one, and we would be foolish to think we could settle it overnight. But as I suggested earlier, what if God wants to partner with us to make things better for the next generation? What if God is uniquely positioning *us* to be the generation that finally gets it right? What if *we* are the ones to have the edge on loving *all* of his children as he does—without measure, margin, or bureaucracy?

How do we get there? What *can* we do? And where do go from here?

There are, I believe, four actions we have to join together to do for the sake of our girls. And I believe that we, as the church, should lead the way in this. Those four actions are to have courageous conversations, to build alliances, to pursue rather than merely permit, and to study and pray.

1. Have courageous conversations.

We have to start having courageous conversations about these topics. A courageous conversation is often an uncomfortable one in which people face their biases and beliefs head on in order to acknowledge a problem or injustice appropriately and address it. But as some wise leaders ahead of me have shown me, courageous conversations are valuable and necessary, too.

Value is not based only on necessity, nor is necessity based solely on value. There are multiple factors at play here; you could say these conversations are helpful, insightful, catalysts for change and that they initiate dialogue. But all such conversations have to start with each person having the courage to say what they think and feel. Until we risk really trusting and loving one another in our churches, workplaces, and homes, we won't be able to tackle problems of injustice and inequality, and that is why we so often feel as if we are spinning our wheels. Leaders must find ways to require and model these kinds of open conversations. Many people are conflict-avoidant or don't want to admit they may have been part of the problem. Until we risk, trust, and love, such courageous conversations won't happen.

In newsrooms I have participated in and led extremely uncomfortable conversations. As the newsroom's leader, colleagues sometimes called me out in those conversations for perpetuating systemic problems that left people feeling as if their voices weren't being heard, let alone valued. I learned that sometimes good intentions hurt people. And I learned what I said and why. I learned the most from uncomfortable conversations. Those conversations kept me up at night digesting what I had heard. I needed that to happen. Notably, I've had those conversations in newsrooms, not in churches.

My familiarity with courageous conversations came as talk about racial injustice started happening among my coworkers. I had colleagues who led conversations about what it was like to be black after the murders of George Floyd and Ahmed Arbury. We actually scheduled "courageous conversation" time with our staff over Zoom at the height of quarantine. We also facilitated a place for people of color to continue conversations without management around. We leaders supported that because we knew having those conversations is how truth is revealed so change can happen.

Perhaps the most courageous conversations happened when I or another leader made a comment that offended someone in an editorial meeting and someone was courageous enough to call us out about it. Out of that came really long editorial meetings in which people spoke freely. Yes, I'd get calls after those meetings from people expressing how uncomfortable they'd felt. But others called and said they'd never before experienced anything so grace-filled and genuine in the workplace.

Perhaps you've engaged in such courageous conversations with your coworkers or in a human resources training session to reshape your work culture. The marketplace is doing this pretty well—not perfectly, but it is making more improvements than I've seen in the church. As the church, we can and should engage in these conversations at work or with friends. But I don't think we should stop there. If you aren't regularly having courageous conversations about racial inequity, gender inequity, the role of women in your church, and Christian nationalism, you likely aren't leading as a Christian. You can't say you are committed to the cross of Jesus Christ and to being his hands and feet here on earth if you stay in a comfortable bubble pretending everything is fine and everyone is being treated the way Jesus would treat them.

There are a lot of coaches and resources to help you learn how to have courageous conversations. The "Lead Change Group" created one method to get you started. It includes five steps:

1. Clarity: be clear.
2. Curiosity, be curious about what the person is saying and their behavior.
3. Coherence, making sure you understand their viewpoint.
4. Congruence, sharing with them your perspective without undermining theirs.
5. Co-create closure.

Those final two steps really focus on ensuring you see each other's view points and are able to take the next productive steps.

Change starts with a conversation. If we're not talking about the undercurrent of gender inequality in our churches and church families, we are doing harm, not good. To do better, we must start talking and listening.

2. Build alliances.

Change does not happen overnight. Change takes work, hard work. The kind of work that can easily cause you to become frustrated because it requires significant support and time to see long-term results.

I was moved from TV station to TV station and city to city because I could make things happen. In fact, I've been described in front of dozens of people as a "change agent." To effect change, you need allies to support you as you fight for change.

ELI is a training company that helps organizations "solve the problem of bad behavior in the workplace." That's how the company describes itself on its website. Look at how they approach workplace allies to effect change:

> Workplace allies are people who are willing to personally align themselves with colleagues to make sure they're heard and included. A workplace ally sees it as their responsibility to keep bad behaviors from happening to anyone. True allies don't just rush in to be the hero in individual cases. Instead, they work for systemic change.[58]

That reminds me of Jesus' disciples. They worked together for systemic change so *everyone* would hear the good news, not just Jews. God's love and gift of grace are available for all.

If you're thinking you're on the outside and not part of the special "clique" at work or church, the idea of creating workplace allies may intimidate you. So here are some ways you can build alliances to bring about change for good.

First, offer support. When you see someone struggling to make some change, offer some support. Ask how you can help. Ask them what they need. Perhaps they need to bounce ideas off someone. Whatever it may be, be there for them.

---

[58] Eli, Inc., "What Does It Mean to be an 'Ally' at Work?" *ELI,* November 21, 2019, https://www.eliinc.com/allies-in-the-workplace/.

Second, share information. Share what you've seen, what you know, what you've learned. Don't hog information that can help drive change. Share it with others.

Third and finally, do not use workplace alliances to spread gossip. The purpose of an alliance is not to create an additional clique: it's to spur change and action. An alliance is not a group of like-minded people who gossip about those who think differently. That will do nothing to help your cause. It will only hurt it—especially for women among whom men may already perceive gossip to be a problem. Gossip stops progress in its tracks.

Earlier, when I mentioned finding "your people," I was talking about finding workplace allies. I think of my discipleship group ladies. We may live in different cities. Some of us work for churches or church-based organizations, while others of us work in the marketplace. We have our differences, for sure. But we have a single goal: to be there for each other so we can be the best kingdom builders possible.

Start with the end in mind. Know what you are called to do together. Our purpose was to be there for one another as we attempted to be the best kingdom builders possible. What's yours? Who are the people who share your purpose? Find them, and form an alliance with them and work toward change together.

If you are frustrated or feel alone, I guarantee someone you know feels the same. Ask that person to join you for lunch or coffee. If you can't think of how to approach the situation, ask God to present the situation to you. I'll never regret the day I agreed to go to lunch with my friend Janie. That was the day I had just gotten on my knees and asked God to show me in a big and bold way how to live out my purpose to serve other women. That moment led to an alliance with Janie and other godly women. Now I'm writing to you and speaking to women across the country. I believe God put the wheels in motion for all that during the lunch with Janie.

Take courage from the promise of Matthew 18:20, that "where two or three gather in my name, there am I with them" (NIV). Gather in his name. He will be there. And his plan will unfold.

3. Pursue; don't merely permit.

Permit: to consent to, expressly or formally.[59]

Pursue: to find or employ measures to obtain or accomplish.[60]

Author and speaker Jen Wilkin wrote an article on her blog about the complementarian view of women in leadership. Complementarianism is the perspective that men and women have different but complementary roles and responsibilities in marriage, family life, and religious leadership. In the article, she said it's one thing to permit women to lead but another to pursue their engagement or to provide them with opportunities to do so.[61] When I read this, it spoke to me so much that I immediately started sharing it. She went on to challenge her readers:

> Do you desire to leverage the equal complementary value of women in your church? Don't give us a chance to ask permission. Get out ahead of us. ... Approach us with what you intend to empower us to do. End the culture of permission and you will dispel the stigma of submission. We are not usurpers; we are the possessors of every capacity you lack and the celebrators of every capacity you possess.[62]

What I particularly love about Wilkin's words is that she addresses the stigma surrounding the issue, not just the issue itself. You see, if you are implying women are allowed to do something but you are not pursuing them to do it, that feeds a stigma that women who are wired to lead can only lead under limitations and only when permission is granted. We know we're not the first choice, is what I'm saying. And we are very aware of it. Trust me. If you find yourself saying, "If she had only spoken up!" you are perpetuating the problem. Why?

[59] *Merriam-Webster Dictionary*, "permit," accessed January 31, 2022, https://www.merriam-webster.com/dictionary/permit.

[60] *Merriam-Webster Dictionary*, "pursue," accessed January 31, 2022, https://www.merriam-webster.com/dictionary/pursue.

[61] Jen Wilkin, "The Complementarian Woman: Permitted or Pursued?" *Jen Wilkin* (blog), April 23, 2013, https://www.jenwilkin.net/blog/2013/04/the-complementarian-woman-permitted-or.html.

[62] Jen Wilkin, *The Complementarian Woman*.

Because a man doesn't have to speak up to lead. Church leaders, you pursue men to lead all the time. You don't even think twice about it. But only rarely do you church leaders pursue a woman for a role for which she is gifted.

So I ask you, dear reader: What are you doing to pursue female leaders in your churches and organizations? What are you doing to pursue young women and prepare them to lead as adults?

Giving permission to women to lead is vastly different than pursuing women to lead. Look again at the definitions above. Pursuing requires that you seek the women you want to lead. Look around you. The person you need to lead others may be right in front of you. And that person may be a woman. Pursue her. Ask her to apply. Encourage her to try. Do your part to create a pathway, then lead her to it.

4. Study and Pray

Greg Nettle, the president of church-planting organization Stadia, explained to me and a group of female leaders that when he was senior pastor of Rivertree Christian Church in Cleveland, Ohio, the church leadership spent seven years studying the roles of women in the church before moving to an egalitarian stance.[63]

I love hearing stories like these about churches that have devoted themselves to praying that the Lord will help them to have eyes and hearts like his toward others. God does his best work in us when we are willing to let him move in our hearts and change our minds.

God commands and invites us to spend time with him. It's only when we dive deeply into his Word and open our hearts and minds to what God is telling us that we can be agents of change.

Study and pray on your own. Study and pray in groups. Study and pray with your friends who are in your bubble. And study and pray with those who are in another bubble. Just think of how we could

---

[63] Greg Nettles, "Leading in High Pressure Environments with Suzanne Nadell," *The Church Planting Podcast with Greg Nettles*, Season 4, Episode 5, July 26, 2021, https://thechurchplantingpodcast.libsyn.com/s4e5-leading-in-high-pressure-environments-wsuzanne-nadell.

show God's love if every bubble kept bursting and the people moved into other bubbles, then those bubbles burst too so that those people could hear and learn from people in yet another bubble. Imagine the understanding we'd gain and the opportunities to show love! All that from studying and praying with people who aren't like us.

God loves you. He wants to spend time with you. He wants you to spend time with community in his name. When you do that, you can hear him. And some amazing things will happen.

Final Thoughts

The last thing I want anyone to assume after reading this book is that I'm bitter toward my family, teachers, upbringing, church leaders, or anyone else who may have failed to do their part to help me over the years. I'm not. I'm grateful for my path and the lessons I've learned. And now I'm grateful to be in a position to share what I've learned with other female leaders, church leaders, and especially young women.

I admit I spent my young adult years resenting the stigma of not being allowed to do certain things in certain circles because of my gender and being expected to do others in which I wasn't particularly interested. But now I realize I missed something God wants me to know every day: that I am complex and wonderfully made. When I embraced that truth, everything else started making sense to me. I had gifts to offer the world and I had a message of God's love and grace to undergird those gifts. I'm better, not bitter, for the path I have taken. But I'll never stop trying to help the church get it right for the next generation. I'll never stop identifying the leadership gifts I see in the young girls I teach in Sunday school. And I'll never stop looking for opportunities to mentor the young women coming up after me in the marketplace.

I'll never stop because I know firsthand how beautifully wonderful and complex God made all his girls and because each and every one has something to offer the world and God's kingdom, whether it be as a homemaker or as a newscaster.

What about you? What will you do to help our girls? If you believe God really has made us all in complex and wonderful ways, isn't it possible he made us all with different gifts—including the potential to lead in his name and for his glory? I challenge you to embrace the leadership potential of the young women around you. If the church can do that, I really believe it's possible our young women won't have to run somewhere else for validation or equipping. Fact-check your Jesus, and maybe our girls and young women won't have to learn these important lessons in a newsroom or other workplace instead of in the church.

Acknowledgements

There are so many people to thank for helping me make this book become a reality.

Chalice Press for understanding the need for this book and for all of their support. Thank you for understanding my vision. Brad Lyons and Ulrike Guthrie, your eyes and wisdom meant so much to me in the process.

Carolyn Reed Master for being my guide and encourager in so many ways. Your focus and direction will always mean more to me than I can express.

My bosses and mentors at Cox Media Group and Cox Enterprises. You contributed to a twenty-five-plus-year career and embraced and celebrate me for who I am. To say that I was a part of working for people like you who have a genuine mission to make this world a better place is an honor.

My discipleship journey ladies. Our two-year journey together was life-changing. You gave me confidence and encouraged me to let the Holy Spirit guide me. I will never take your friendship for granted.

My church families. As I bounced around the country, church families in nearly every city embraced me and gave me opportunities to lead, be it in Sunday school, among women, or even as a lead team member and elder. You were my home away from home.

Mom and Dad. You raised a strong girl and allowed her to be herself and dream. The seeds you planted in me to serve and lead have blossomed.

Michael and Price. Not only have you sacrificed as I climbed the newsroom ladder over the years, but you've cared for me in times of illness, listened to my concerns and dreams, and inspired me to be a better person every day. This book would not have been possible without your love, patience, and encouragement. I love you both.

And my Father in heaven. Thank you for making me a unique masterpiece. Thank you, Holy Spirit, for nudging me to take a giant leap of faith. And thank you, Jesus, for the life lessons you taught us so we can teach others.

Bibliography

Allen, Marshall. "The Biblical Guide to Reporting." *The New York Times*. September 1, 2018. https://www.nytimes.com/2018/09/01/opinion/christianity-bible-journalism.html.

Andrews, Shawn. "Why Women Don't Always Support Other Women." *Forbes*. January 21, 2020. https://www.forbes.com/sites/forbescoachescouncil/2020/01/21/why-women-dont-always-support-other-women/?sh=80762363b05b.

Andrus, Danielle. "Pandemic Driving Up Employee Burnout Rates: Employees Feel Responsible." *Benefits Pro*. October 20, 2020. https://www.benefitspro.com/2020/10/20/pandemic-driving-up-employee-burnout-rates-managers-feel-responsible/?slreturn=20210729181635.

Associated Press-NORC. "A New Way of Looking at Trust in the Media: Do Americans Share Journalism's Core Values?" April 14, 2021. https://apnorc.org/projects/a-new-way-of-looking-at-trust-in-media-do-americans-share-journalisms-core-values/.

Bateman, Nicole, and Martha Ross. "Why Has Covid-19 Been Especially Harmful for Working Women?" *Brookings*. October 2020. https://www.brookings.edu/essay/why-has-covid-19-been-especially- harmful-for-working-women/.

Bauder, David. "Study Finds People Want More than Watchdogs for Journalists." *AP News*. April 14, 2021. https://apnews.com/article/politics-media-tom-rosenstiel-journalists-915025bcab8f5910381eee11b5cb9d17.

Be the Bridge. "About Be the Bridge." Accessed January 29, 2022. https://bethebridge.com/about/.

Brenan, Megan. "Americans No Longer Prefer Male Boss to Female Boss." *Gallup*. November 16, 2017. https://news.gallup.com/poll/222425/americans-no-longer-prefer-male-boss-female-boss.aspx.

Caldwell, Gilbert H. "Christians Should Defend Journalists." *UM News.* October 28, 2019. https://www.umnews.org/en/news/christians-should-defend-journalists.

City-Data. "Neoga, Illinois Income Map, Earnings Map, and Wages Data." Accessed January 31, 2022. https://www.city-data.com/income/income-Neoga-Illinois.html.

Clark, Maria. "70+ Sexual Harassment in the Workplace Statistics." *Etacktics.* November 4, 2021. https://etactics.com/blog/sexual-harassment-in-the-workplace-statistics.

Cloud, Henry, and John Townsend. *Boundaries: When to Say Yes, How to Say No to Take Control of Your Life.* Grand Rapids: Zondervan, 1992.

Cole, Kadi. *Developing Female Leaders: Navigate the Minefields and Release the Potential of Women in Your Church.* Nashville: Thomas Nelson, 2019.

Connley, Courtney. "A Record 41 Women are Fortune 500 CEOs—and for the First Time Two Black Women Made the List." *CNBC.* June 2, 2021. https://www.cnbc.com/2021/06/02/fortune-500-now-has-a-record-41-women-running-companies.html#:~:text=A%20record%2041.

Costigan, Amelia. "The Double-Bind Dilemma for Women in Leadership." *Catalyst.* August 2, 2018. https://www.catalyst.org/research/infographic-the-double-bind-dilemma-for-women-in-leadership/.

Craver, Jack. "Has the Internet Killed Sick Days?" *Benefits Pro.* January 18, 2019. https://www.benefitspro.com/2019/01/18/has-the-internet-killed-sick-days/.

Dowland, Seth. "The 'Modesto Manifesto.'" *Christian History Magazine* 111 (2014). https://christianhistoryinstitute.org/magazine/article/the-modesto-manifesto/.

Eli, Inc. "What Does It Mean to be an 'Ally' at Work?" *ELI* (blog). November 21, 2019. https://www.eliinc.com/allies-in-the-workplace/.

Ettman, Catherine K., Salma M. Abdalla, and Gregory Cohen. "Prevalence of Depression Symptoms in US Adults before

and during the Covid-19 Pandemic." Boston University
School of Public Health. September 2, 2020. DOI:
10.1001/jamanetworkopen.2020.19686.

Ewing-Nelson, Claire, and Jasmine Tucker. "A Year into the
Pandemic, Women are Still Short 5.1 Million Jobs."
National Women's Law Center. March 2021. https://nwlc.
org/wp-content/uploads/2021/03/Feb-Jobs-Day-v2.pdf.

Feldblum, Chai R., and Victoria A. Lipnic. "Select Task Force
on the Study of Harassment in the Workplace." *U.S.
Equal Employment Opportunity Commission.* June 2016.
https://www.eeoc.gov/select-task-force-study-harassment-
workplace#_ftn16.

Felton, Julia. "5 Steps to Having Courageous Conversations."
Lead Change. October 20, 2017. https://leadchangegroup.
com/5-steps-to-having-courageous-conversations/.

Fickel, Julie. "Burnout in Pastors and Church Leadership."
M1Psychology. Accessed January 31, 2022. https://
m1psychology.com/burnout-in-pastors-and-church-
leadership/.

Goleman, Daniel. "Sexual Harassment: It's About Power, Not
Lust." *The New York Times.* October 22, 1991. www.
nytimes.com/1991/10/22/science/sexual-harassment-it-s-
about-power-not-lost.html.

Green, Emma. "The Tiny Blond Bible Teacher Taking On the
Evangelical Political Machine." *The Atlantic.* October 2018.
https://www.theatlantic.com/magazine/archive/2018/10/
beth-moore-bible-study/568288/.

Keller, Gary, and Jay Papsan, *The ONE Thing: The Surprisingly
Simple Truth Behind Extraordinary Results.* Austin: Bend
Press, 2012.

Korman, Hailly T.N., Bonnie O'Keefe, and Matt Repka. "Missing
in the Margins 2020: Estimating the Scale of the Covid-19
Attendance Crisis." *Bellweather Education Partners.*
October 21, 2020. https://bellwethereducation.org/
publication/missing-margins-estimating-scale-covid-19-
attendance-crisis.

Lapidot-Lefler, Noam, and Azy Barak. "Effects of Anonymity, Invisibility, and Lack of Eye Contact on Toxic Online Disinhibition." *Computers in Human Behavior* 28, no. 2 (March 2012).

Lifeway Research. "Most Teenagers Drop Out of Church When They Become Young Adults." January 15, 2019. https://lifewayresearch.com/2019/01/15/most-teenagers-drop-out-of-church-as-young-adults/.

Martino, Jessica, Jennifer Pegg, and Elizabeth Pegg Frates. "The Connection Prescription: Using the Power of Social Interactions and the Deep Desire for Connectedness to Empower Health and Wellness." *American Journal of Lifestyle Medicine* 11, no. 6 (November-December 2017). https://www.ncbi.nlm.nih.gov/pmc/articles/PMC6125010/.

Maxwell, John C. *The Complete 101 Collection: What Every Leader Needs to Know.* Nashville: Thomas Nelson, 2010.

"Martin Luther King Jr. The Most Segregated Hour in America." *Meet the Press.* April 17, 1960. Posted April 29, 2014. YouTube video. https://www.youtube.com/watch?v=1q881g1L_d8.

Milford Morse, Michelle. "Women Are Being Pushed out of the Workforce. The Private Sector Must Do More to Address This Crisis." *United Nations Foundations* (blog). March 18, 2021. https://unfoundation.org/blog/post/women-are-being-pushed-out-of-the-workforce-the-private-sector-must-do-more-to-address-this-crisis/.

Minar, Barbara. *Unrealistic Expectations: Capturing the Thief of a Woman's Joy.* Wheaton: Victor Books, 1990.

Modestino, Alicia Sasser. "Coronavirus Child-care Crisis Will Set Women Back a Generation." *The Washington Post.* July 29, 2020. https://www.washingtonpost.com/us-policy/2020/07/29/childcare-remote-learning-women-employment/.

Moore, Beth. *Chasing Vines: Finding Your Way to an Immensely Fruitful Life.* Carol Stream: Tyndale, 2020.

Nettles, Greg, host. "Leading in High Pressure Environments with Suzanne Nadell." *The Church Planting Podcast with Greg Nettles.* July 26, 2021. https://thechurchplantingpodcast. libsyn.com/s4e5-leading-in-high-pressure-environments-wsuzanne-nadell.

Ortberg, John. *If You Want to Walk on Water, You Have to Get out of the Boat.* Grand Rapids: Zondervan, 2001.

———. *The Me I Want to Be.* Grand Rapids: Zondervan, 2010.

Pew Research Center. "In U.S., Decline of Christianity Continues at Rapid Pace: An Update on America's Changing Religious Landscape." October 17, 2019. https://www. pewforum.org/2019/10/17/in-u-s-decline-of-christianity-continues-at-rapid-pace/.

———. "U.S. Teen Take After Their Parents Religiously, Attend Services Together and Enjoy Family Rituals." September 10, 2020. https://www.pewforum.org/2020/09/10/what-do-parents-want-for-their-teens/.

Poorman Richards, Sue, and Lawrence O. Richards. *Women of the Bible: The Life and Times of Every Woman in the Bible.* Nashville: Thomas Nelson, 2003.

Ro, Christine. "Why Do We Still Distrust Women Leaders?" *BBC.* January 19, 2021. https://www.bbc.com/worklife/ article/20210108-why-do-we-still-distrust-women-leaders.

Rode, Joseph C., Marne L. Arthuad-Day, and Aarti Ramaswami. "A Time-Lagged Study of Emotional Intelligence and Salary." *Journal of Vocational Behavior* (May 2017). DOI: 10.1016/j.jvb.2017.05.001.

Ruhl, Charlotte. "Implicit Unconscious Bias." *Simply Psychology.* July 1, 2020. https://www.simplypsychology.org/implicit-bias.html.

Sandberg, Cheryl. *Lean In: Women, Work, and the Will to Lead.* New York: Alfred A. Knopf, 2013.

Society of Professional Journalists. "SPJ Code of Ethics." Revised September 6, 2014. https://www.spj.org/ethicscode. asp#:~:text=Preamble%20Members%20of%20the%20 Society%20of%20Professional%20Journalists,and%20 thorough.%20An%20ethical%20journalist%20acts%20 with%20integrity.

Stanley, Andy. *Better Decisions, Fewer Regrets: 5 Questions to Help You Determine Your Next Move.* Grand Rapids: Zondervan, 2020.

Underwood, Doug. *From Yahweh to Yahoo! The Religious Roots of the Secular Press.* Champaign: University of Illinois Press, 2002.

U.S. Bureau of Labor Statistics. "Highlights of Women's Earnings in 2019." December 2020. https://www.bls.gov/opub/ reports/womens-earnings/2019/pdf/home.pdf.

Vogels, Emily A. "Some Digital Divides Persist between Rural, Urban, and Suburban America." *Pew Research Center.* August 19, 2021. https://www.pewresearch.org/fact-tank/2021/08/19/some-digital-divides-persist-between-rural-urban-and-suburban-america/.

Warren, Rick. *The Purpose Driven Life: What on Earth Am I Here For?* Grand Rapids: Zondervan, 2002.

Whitaker, Bill. "Brené Brown: The 60 Minutes Interview." *60 Minutes.* March 29, 2020. https://www.cbs.com/shows/60_ minutes/video/KtGPyuGc9k6DeI_8QDbYa7acA15FCgG t/brene-brown-the-60-minutes-interview/.

Jen Wilkin. "The Complementarian Woman: Permitted or Pursued?" *Jen Wilkin* (blog). April 23, 2013. https://www. jenwilkin.net/blog/2013/04/the-complementarian-woman-permitted-or.html.

———. *Women of the Word.* Wheaton: Crossway Publishing, 2014.

Williams, Melissa J. "The Price Women Pay for Assertiveness and How to Minimize It." *The Wall Street Journal.* May 30, 2016. https://www.wsj.com/articles/the-price-women-leaders-pay-for-assertivenessand-how-to-minimize-it-1464660240.

YPulse. "These Are the Top Places Gen Z & Millennials Say They Find Community." April 20, 2021. https://www.ypulse. com/article/2021/04/20/these-are-the-top-places-gen-z-millennials-say-they-find-community/.

"100 Social Media Statistics You Must Know in 2022." *Status Brew* (blog). December 9, 2021. https://statusbrew.com/insights/ social-media-statistics/#global-social-media-statistics.

About the Author

With an extraordinary 30-year career in journalism, Suzanne Nadell has led some of the nation's leading newsrooms, including WSB-TV, one of the top local TV stations in the country. Since Suzanne returned to WSB-TV as News Director in 2019, the station has brought home dozens of Emmy Awards, regional Edward R. Murrow Awards, and a Gracie Award, which recognizes women in media.

Prior to WSB, Nadell led the news team at WPXI in Pittsburgh. In her time there, she led the station to new ratings heights. The station's 11:00 p.m. newscast ranked as the highest rated late newscast among the largest television markets. WPXI also brought home ten Mid-Atlantic Chapter Emmy Awards and a regional Edward R. Murrow award for best newscast.

Nadell has also worked as the news director of KOKI in Tulsa, Oklahoma. Under her leadership, in just three years the station went from third to first in adult viewers aged twenty-five to fifty-four. The station also received a national Edward R. Murrow for best newscast, six regional Edward R. Murrow awards, and ten regional Emmy Awards.

Nadell has also worked as an executive producer at WSB-TV in Atlanta, and as a producer at WFLA-TV in Tampa, WFTV in Orlando, and WBBH in Fort Myers.

Her career started at WJHL in Johnson City, Tennessee, as a production assistant, producer, and reporter.

Nadell received a BA in communications from Milligan College, in Johnson City, Tennessee. She and her husband, Michael, have a teenaged son named Price. They are active members of Atlanta Christian Church and live in Brookhaven, Georgia.

Reach out to Suzanne online:

Website   Suzannenadell.com

Instagram   @suznadell

Facebook   Suzanne Nadell